STEALING LIVES

LIVES

*Systemic Child Abuse and the Smokescreens
of Organised Vatican Criminality*

First published in the UK by Nec Laudibus Nec Timore Publishing

Copyright © Rafael Viola and Countess Sigrid von Galen, 2022, Nuneaton/London

The rights of Rafael Viola and Countess Sigrid von Galen to be identified as the authors of this work have been asserted by them in accordance with the Copyright, Designs & Patents Act 1988.

A copy of the British Library Cataloguing in Publication Data is available from the British Library.

Paperback ISBN: 978-1-7394220-0-4
eBook ISBN: 978-1-7394220-1-1

Printed and bound in the UK

STEALING LIVES

Systemic Child Abuse and the Smokescreens of Organised Vatican Criminality

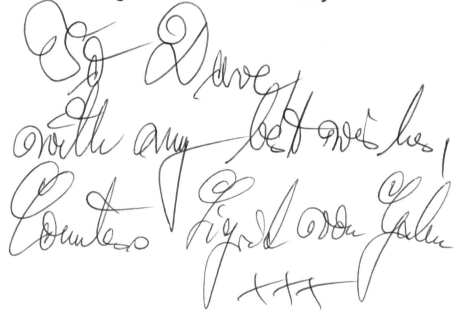

To Dave, with my best wishes, Countess Sigrid von Galen xxx

A Survivors and Whistleblowers' Perspective and its Lessons by

COUNTESS SIGRID VON GALEN
AND RAFAEL VIOLA

For all Survivors of child abuse, sexual and otherwise, and their families and friends, whose lives were stolen and hijacked by the Roman Catholic and Anglican Church and other religious and state Institutions

Contents

Foreword

Rafael Viola's story tells the trauma of so many, and by sharing it, he gives those, who are still suffering in silence, his voice until they are also ready to finally come forward to tell theirs.

Many victims were not heard or only insufficiently assisted and in the end let down by various inquiries, safeguarding teams and church hierarchy.

The papal nuncio, the Pope himself, cardinals, arch/bishops, nuns and clergy failed them entirely except for non-committal broken promises and empty words.

It is appalling that victims were not looked after appropriately even and especially by the IICSA, which was a highly selective inquiry with numerous survivors left out in the cold and those, who took part in the testimonies, were largely retraumatised and felt let down in the end and even more silenced than ever, as many institutions simply got away even with murder…

Rafael, like others, had to face a huge group of clergy, lawyers of the churches, bishops and officials in the same room, who either ignored the survivors or intimidated them by their sheer arrogance.

Some survivors were not even able to get home again after a long triggering inquiry session and relied on the kindness of other survivors to offer them to share a room and get them food, whilst lawyers and clergy were paid fees and accommodation.

The Institute for Criminology and Justice wants to make the testimonies of survivors heard and has written its own independent report on request of Croome Court survivors, which is also to be found in parts in this book, as Rafael wants to make the patterns of organised abuse and other church criminality and their cover ups and the Omertà culture visible that comes with it.

Thus this book is not just about telling Rafael's story but also takes a wider look at the bigger picture of organised church crimes and their cover ups worldwide, and connects the dots from many angles and perspectives, including the various international inquiries into Child Sexual Abuse, and how they were sabotaged by the churches in many ways.

The accounts of his experiences are heartbreaking and triggering for many survivors - so, take your time and if you can, spread the testimony.

Every voice counts! Be the next one to amplify 'F49', Rafael Viola's voice and with his story also the shared trauma of so many others yet unheard survivors.

Together we can bring justice through exposure of what the perpetrator institutions wanted to be forgotten and classified! Thank you for listening and spreading the truth

Countess Sigrid von Galen

Chapter 1: Introduction

I am Rafael Viola. A Whistleblower.

My name is Rafael Viola. I am a whistleblower. I have assisted the police and BBC journalists in investigations into the crimes of The Sisters of Charity of St Paul the Apostle at Croome Court, the De La Salle Brothers at St Gilbert's School and the staff at Tennal Assessment Centre.

I contacted other survivors and helped them get legal representation. There's about 50 survivors of violent abuses at Croome Court that I know of, and there will be many, many more.

There are two allegations of murder against the nuns and allegations of sexual abuse by the nuns and male staff and considerable evidence of physical and psychological torture.

And yet, to date, there has been no proper investigation into those crimes. I think that's a crime in itself.

I was made an Ambassador to the Independent Inquiry into Child Sexual Abuse.

I attended the hearings on the understanding that I would be heard.

This was my chance to get the truth of the scale of abuse that we, as children, suffered on the record. I am disabled. I use a wheelchair.

I've had a triple heart bypass and I struggle with vascular problems and post-traumatic stress disorder every day. Nevertheless, I travelled to London, sat through day after day of the IICSA hearings to be told, eventually, we would not be heard, after all.

I was understandably furious. As a result, I ended up having an angina attack and spent the night at St Thomas' Hospital.

No one from the inquiry even called to find out how I was.

I still had to fight. I told them that the inquiry was a farce. I told my lawyer he was a double agent. They decided to read out a two minute summary of my statement.

That was it. And then they moved on. No mention of my recommendations. It was insulting. It felt like our very painful, traumatic experiences did not matter to them.

There were so many sneaky moves.

There's a lot of things that need to be exposed, especially the way the IICSA inquiry mistreated survivors.

I was doing alright until then.

Afterwards, I was done. I ended up having a nervous breakdown. I found out later that the barrister representing me was actually only a property lawyer.

I wouldn't have gone if I had known that. He hardly communicated with me.

I didn't even meet him in person. Our expectations were seriously mismanaged.

I feel used by the Inquiry. It was re-traumatising. What was the point in that?

To date, I have received five apologies from the Roman Catholic Church.

Three from The Archbishop of Birmingham, one from Cardinal

Nichols and one from the Papal Nuncio.

Those apologies were accompanied by promises

to help me, but they have not helped me. My daughters have chased them up by email and now they do not even reply.

I understand that is known as

stonewalling. The Tablet reported that the Papal Nuncio's meeting with us was a marked change in approach.

We were reported as being cautiously optimistic

at the time. Not anymore.

The actual truth, which was not fully heard at the Inquiry, is this:

I was born in Glasgow on the 21 July 1959 to a multicultural Catholic family.

My parents were Maria and Alexander Viola. I had eight siblings, and we grew up in a very rough area. Money was quite tight, but we were fed and clothed well.

My father was quite strict but not abusive in any way. This is a photo of me when I was seven, when I was still living mostly at home with my family in Glasgow.

© Rafael Viola

If you are truly interested, you are invited now to read the full story.

Chapter 2:

Childhood Fragments

I was thrust into this life, when my poor mother went into labour suddenly and just about made it to the bathroom, screaming to my sleeping father to get help from the neighbours.

He was exhausted after a long day's work and lulled from the obligatory after work pint but was instantly dragged out of bed by her alarming voice.

I was still attached to the navel cord around my neck, blue all over, jaundiced and me and my family probably traumatised for life from my dramatic entrance into the world.

What can I say? When the way of birth is anything to go by my life was set to survive even the life and death challenges from the beginning!

My name is Rafael Viola, I am 64 years old, and I am a survivor of sexual abuse at the hands of the Catholic church. It was only 10 years ago where I **admitted this, confronted this** and **began the journey of healing and dealing with my suppressed emotions**.

But today was not a good day, today my trauma, my experience, my sadness was evaluated and quantified to a figure that has disparaged me once again. The price of my robbed childhood, the abuse I endured, and negligence that the Roman Catholic Church lawyers suggested as compensation. A deplorable evaluation of my existence that I won't even mention, as it won't even cover a lifetime of lost education!

How can we survivors heal when these criminal perpetrators still treat us in deniability and utmost limitation to their liability as worthless incompetent degenerates? The church still commits and covers up abuse worldwide under abuse of immunity, with governments allowing them to investigate their own organised criminality?!

Being free from harm and abuse should be a fundamental human right for children.

Especially as children, we are supposed to be protected and kept safe. My childhood memories outside my family had none of this but consisted of threats, name calling, abandonment, suicide attempts, sexual abuse, humiliation and bullying to name but a few. This I have carried with me for most of my life in silence keeping it locked up inside me.

My time at Croome Court can only be described as the worst time of my life and upon reflection I have endured some very dark times after that, too.

At the age of 10 you are supposed to be transitioning into pre-adolescent stages and the brain is rapidly growing and learning. What I learnt at the age of 10 was not like normal 10-year-olds. I learnt mainly to survive in an extreme environment of psychological warfare, deceit, abuse and violence in every way by emotionally detaching from life, and not trusting anyone, and to fear everyone around me.

Until one day it had all got too much, and I tried to end my life. At ten years of age, I wanted out for good. On release from Croome Court for the holiday I had taken Valium from my father for his treatment of TB.

I took 21 of these tiny yellow tablets in the hope I would die. The next thing I remember was waking up in hospital erratic and angry that my plan had failed because I was still alive. It made me feel powerless and I wanted to scream.

Medical staff even documented in my paperwork that this suicide attempt was a result of me not wanting to attend Croome Court and there was a high risk of me attempting again if I was to return. This was dismissed and back to Croome Court I went, after I tried in vain to plead with my father, who had been threatened with legal action and even prison, should he prevent me from returning to Croome Court.

Such was the power and the long arm of the Roman Catholic Church. My late friend John Lamb, who was an orphan in Croome Court, even reported a murder by nuns to the police, only to be returned to the very nuns he witnessed to murder and who did bury another abused boy there.

Never did I imagine I would have to go through all of this process to find justice and closure. Initially I just wanted to proceed with a civil claim via my lawyer and be done with it. I didn't expect to be enrolled into schemes or to have been part of inquiries and to be meeting religious figures like the Archbishop of Birmingham and the Papal Nuncio.

Although this has sometimes felt like never ending and distressing, I am proud of the accomplishments I have made, the people I have met through this path and the voice I have found. As I have got older the abuse had eaten away at me and had consumed me like a virus.

It goes without saying that I had times in my life where I felt restless and couldn't continue my life as it was any longer, as I carried all the burden of my haunting past on my own. I couldn't tell my wife and only told my daughters after my wife had passed away.

I felt then it was time to speak out and I am thankful now that we live in a world where there are multiple effective social media platforms to be heard and the subject of historical abuse is starting to feel intolerable even to wider society and is no longer deemed taboo when spoken about.

The following extract below is part of my statement that I had prepared with my lawyer at the time:

9. My mother was Maria Viola, and my father was Alexander Viola. My grandparents were a mix of Irish, Spanish and Italian, the latter being the source of which the name Viola comes from. I had eight siblings, and we grew up in an area I would describe as rough. Money was quite tight, but we were fed and clothed. My father was quite strict but not abusive in any way..

10. In Scotland, I attended a number of residential schools, because my family was too large for me to be cared for at home.

I was never treated badly in any of those. I do not remember the name of the school, as I was very young at the time, but I went there for two 3-month periods, I think.

11. We then moved to Coventry when I was nine. The reason for moving was that my dad needed to work. He mainly worked in landscape gardening.

12. When I arrived in Coventry I was sent to St Ann's Primary School, in Coventry. It was a fairly regular Catholic primary school. I had found it hard to settle in, and I had played truant a number of times.

13. Playing truant got me in trouble with the social services, and I was eventually sent to Croome Court because I was judged to be mentally retarded by Coventry social services. I was then described in a school report (I cannot remember which school) by an RG Robinson, the Headteacher, as being from a "deteriorating" home. I believe this had an influence on the decision to put me into care.

14. In approximately 1969 when I was ten I was sent to Croome Court. I was told I was moving by my social worker, but I do not remember his name. I was not under a care order before that point, but my mother had been forced to sign a document giving me up to social services to be placed in Croome Court. She had signed it not being aware of what it was, as she was Spanish and did not speak very much English.

15. The Council's educational psychologist, MF Brittain, prepared a report on me, on the subject of my "non-attendance" at school, and stating that I had a reading age of *seven* years when I was eleven. On this basis they said I was severely *retarded* and that I was suffering from the *"stultifying effects of a particularly deprived cultural background"*.

16. They also said my *"linguistic background in itself is enough to cause retardation",* referencing my multicultural and multilingual parents, and mentioned a *"very unsettled home life"*.

17. Therefore they recommended I attend "a residential school for educationally subnormal children."

18. It was recommended, therefore, that I was sent to BesfordCourt.

19. I think I was committed to the care of social services at that point. I am not sure however as I do not have a document which states this, and I cannot remember being placed under a care order. However, from this point, it felt that social services had a greater say in my life, for example when I ran *a*way, and social services chose to keep me in Croome Court against my parents' wishes.

Me and my dog Rickie, © Rafael Viola

Chapter 3:

Childhood in Glasgow

I have overall quite happy memories of my childhood in Glasgow. Despite the poverty and hardship of the post-war era there was a deep sense of sharing and caring in the community. We children were content playing with whatever everyday treasures came literally our way.

It was still the time of rationing, clothes and items were recycled and mended. All families were in the same boat and shared skills, food, and good will to survive.

To us the destruction around us in our neighbourhood in the Gorbals of Glasgow was our playground and brought us also further afield to gather things like bottles, copper, bric-a-brac from the bins of the wealthy neighbourhoods. We lived facing Coal Hill.

I was part of a large Catholic family, used to seeing priests and nuns around in the area and visiting people in our homes. They were part of the community and people trusted them without any reservations.

My mother was a devout Catholic from Spain, and my father a British Officer, who had been stationed in Gibraltar, where he married my mother. She was a very kind lady and my father was quite strict but caring and never abusive or violent.

I would walk every day and roam around for hours with my loyal friend, my dog Rickie, who was half-Labrador, half Alsatian. We would go on adventure tours and discover bird nests and explored empty buildings close to the local distillery on Mary Hill that were inhabited by drunken rats that looked like inflated cats, when they had sampled the whiskey and fell over each other.I used to poke them with a stick to part them as my pastime and entertainment and watch them find their way out of their erratic movements.

Another happy memory is my dad taking me on his shoulders on the way to the bus that would bring us to every Celtic Football Club game. What a treat that was!

The Gorbals was a very deprived immigrant area in Glasgow, with predominantly Italian, Spanish, Pakistani immigrants and Scottish communities mingled together. My grandfather Umberto Viola arrived in Glasgow just after WWI, when he was ten years of age, and my father Alexander was already born in Glasgow.

They ran an ice cream parlour, and my father had a good education, which was paid for by my great grandparents. He joined the Royal Artillerie and was stationed in Gibraltar, where he met my mother. She came from a border town called La Linea dela Concepcion.

My older brother, Alexander, was born there in a military hospital. My parents got married in Gibraltar and then moved to Glasgow in 1949.

We were nine siblings, of whom six are still alive and our dog, Rickie, so it was a buzzing household. I was the seventh child. My mother didn't speak English at all, although my father tried everything to let us grow up in English. She found it too hard but we were brought up in English and spoke the local accent nonetheless.

My Primary School was Our Lady of Assumption for four years. I still remember the first day, when we had to register and our names were called out. Most boys were called James or John - Rafael was very unusual and so, from day 1, I was picked upon and made fun of.

Chapter 4:

Move to England - Shock to the System

Glasgow was a tough place to bring up a family. The outlook to a future without poverty and hunger and with a decent education was almost unimaginable and next to non-existent. My father was looking for better work with improved conditions attached.

Therefore, when I was nine years old, my parents decided to move to England in the hope to give us children a better chance in life. My father was mainly working as a landscape gardener in Coventry.

I attended St Ann's Primary School in Coventry. It was a typical Catholic school but it was difficult for me, as the English curriculum was so different from the Scottish system. We had to take assessment tests and were classified.

I found it very hard to settle in there due to the constant bullying, name calling and mockery of my accent and name in particular. The pressure I felt to adapt to this new setting caused me to play truant several times. I just couldn't face the hostility of the other children and teachers.

Because of my Glaswegian accent and my mother's Spanish background, I was unjustly labelled as 'deprived at home', 'properly damaged', 'severely retarded', and the language barrier was decided to be too big than to leave me in St Ann's Primary School.

Nowadays the same negative attributes would translate into positive ones like 'multilingual', 'multicultural' - but back in those days it was recommended that I would be sent to 'a residential school for educationally subnormal children'.

I was then put under a care order that my mother was bullied into signing and that placed me into the care of Croome Court.

I know now from exchanging information with other survivors from Croome Court and the various institutions that I was sent to that children like me were simply classified to isolate them from their families and to put us into a supply chain for abuse in Roman Catholic institutions for all sorts of reasons and purposes, many with a hidden agenda.

It was a whole supply system that was run, facilitated and covered up by the religious orders, especially the Sisters of Charity of St Paul the Apostle but also by clergy, the police and local authorities of the time.

In one institution I was probably also exposed to illegal experiments with drugs and psychological warfare, as I do not recollect any memories at all from that time. We come back to this in more depth a bit later.

I was put into the Home Office system into the care of St Gilbert's as well, as my truancy got me noticed by Social Services. After I played truant once too often there as well, as I was frightened, I was brought to Croome Court, when I was 9 ½ years, in 1969.

My parents on their wedding day, © Rafael Viola

Chapter 5:

Croome Court - A Hell Hole

Croome Court - The Catholic Gateway to Hell, © Countess Sigrid von Galen

Croome Court was a residential school run by The Sisters of Charity of St Paul the Apostle under the supervision of the Archdiocese of Birmingham. Officially, it was described as a school for 'retarded and disabled children'. The nuns were extremely cruel to us children and subjected us to constant degradation, violence and physical and psychological abuse.

They actually made a lot of money out of us children and are by no means the only Catholic order that is involved in organised child abuse, trafficking and illegal experimentation. They charged even back then £ 400 per child per annum to Social Services.

Before I was brought to Croome Court I was almost looking forward to going there. After all, I was told that I would be looked after by nuns, and my parents being good old fashioned Catholics, hoped that I would thrive there and I thought it would be lovely to be safe with other children in the country in a big mansion.

I was informed by my social worker in Coventry, whose name I can't recall, that I would be signed into care of Croome Court. I was nine and a half years old then. He made my mother sign the papers, although she did not speak English well enough to understand what it was about, and so she signed me effectively over to the authorities.

The council's educational psychologist, MF Brittain, wrote a report on me stating that I had a reading age of seven years, and classifying me as 'severely retarded' and that I was 'suffering from the stultifying effects of a particularly deprived cultural background'.

The report also said that my 'linguistic background in itself is enough to cause retardation', referencing my multicultural and multilingual parents, and mentioned a 'very unsettled home life'.

We know by now that the Catholic church used these kinds of descriptions all over the world to gain access to children for money with corrupt officials in social services and the courts facilitating organised abuse, enforced placements and adoptions and illegal experimentation.

They would pick on children from underprivileged and diverse backgrounds, label them according to the Catholic residential care homes' specifications, who would then groom, sell and abuse the children for their own sadistic purposes but also as mercenaries.

They would often be paid bribery and secret funds given for illegal transactions. We were also sent on begging sprays like in Charles Dickens stories, only that the nuns were taking the position of Fagin.

I remember arriving: Nuns picked seven or eight of us children up from Birmingham New Street Station. From Pershore we were brought to

Croome Court. It was already dark and I was amazed by the long driveway that seemed endless. I could only see the building, once we were already close.

The main building was actually not in use and locked up. We were directly taken to the stables that were transformed into dormitories and class rooms.

We were led up to the dormitories in the dark. Imagine: It was a bitterly cold winter night, no heating, no light - a hell hole! I still remember the eerie smell of fear, the sweat of terror and the damp mixture of mould and beds that had been wet from anxiety.

And there, in the dormitory, in front of 30 metal beds with coarse sheets and blankets stood the stone faced intimidating Mother Superior of Croome Court. She made us take off all our clothes and put them into a box in the centre of the dormitory.

There were also five nuns all around us, who terrified us. They handed us itchy coarse pyjama-like suits with numbers on them, socks and wellies. I remember we all felt so cold and were shivering, with chapped lips.

We were then told 'THE RULES', and that they were God's rules, which basically meant that if we broke the rules we would be extremely severely punished.

One of the rules was that the clothes we were given were the only ones and that we must treat them well and with respect, as we would have no change of clothes.

I felt instantly imprisoned and captured in my own version of an Oliver Twist nightmare, only the nuns were the criminal ringleaders, who even would later send us into the village to go begging, just like Fagin. The nuns, especially the Mother Superior, were all extremely hostile and vile.

They made us kneel on the cold and hard wooden floor and pray. That night I cried myself into sleep. I was utterly scared and frightened to death.

In the morning, we had to kneel again on the floor and pray. Then we were led to the breakfast assembly and we had to line up for our portions of porridge. Sometimes we would be given an egg or a sausage and two slices of bread and a thin watery milky tea.

Afterwards there would be kneeling on the floor and prayers again before school began. Right on the first day I was already in trouble, as I made the mistake to challenge the nun, who tested us and threw words at us to test our vocabulary,

I thought that this was ridiculous, as I felt bored and underchallenged, and thus volunteered a whole sentence. Instantly, the nun would make me kneel facing the wall and saying sharply: 'Oh, you are the clever one, are you?!' Then she hit me with a stick.

All I wanted was to get away from this evil place. The nuns constantly abused us children, called us sadistic names, and beat us up. They tortured us mentally and physically and we were all traumatised from day 1.

There was constant violence from the nuns, priests and the teaching staff. Even when we went on walks into the woods, they would take canes with them and hit us like cattle and call us names again.

We were totally isolated from the outside world. Nobody, except for visiting priests, who would abuse us, too, ever came to Croome Court. The nearest road was far away and one could only very occasionally hear a car from a distance. This sound was like the smell of freedom for me - it made me breathe freely and take me away for a moment in time.

One day, the nuns and staff took us out for once to play in the fields and we were so happy. That was the only time we would not be hit or screamed at, as the nuns were receiving the inspectors from Social Services and wanted as many of us as far away from the visitors as possible. So, we actually never got to speak to anybody and they wrote their assessments without ever having seen us, simply relying on the reports of the nuns.

One or two nuns were showing a hint of compassion but they would soon be moved again to another institution and did not last there very long. One day I was caught smoking a cigarette stump, a habit that I already had as a young boy in the Gorbals, when we picked the stumps up from the ground.

I did not even deny it, when the nun challenged me but nothing prepared me for her viciousness, when she grabbed me by my hair and dragged me up the stairs to the Mother Superior.

I thought they were going to kill me, as the Mother Superior started to beat me up with fury. Then the other nun dragged me to the kitchen, where she drowned my head in a full kitchen sink and waterboarded me again and again and again.

Then they lined us all up again to make an example of me in front of the other boys, and all the nuns came with a cane to beat me in front of 150 children. The fear was so big that you could have heard a pin drop.

The nuns would usually hit us also, if we made the slightest noise during the daily two hour 'recreation time'. Then they would let us kneel facing the wall, hitting us and calling us names randomly.

Sometimes they would make us kneel all night with crossed arms and if we fell asleep or made the slightest move, we would be beaten up again. At other times, the nuns and staff would drag the boys onto the kitchen tables and hold them down in a group and beat them up collectively. The kitchen was filled with horrendous screams and violent abuse.

I was meanwhile much more toughened up, although never violent despite all the violence they used against me. When I was beaten or waterboarded I tried not to cry or to give into the humiliation but stayed as calm as possible, which, of course, the nuns interpreted as a provocation and used it as an excuse to hit me even harder for the resistance.

On several occasions they even put me in a storage board overnight, after I had tried to run away five or six times and was brought back each time, after being caught begging at the bus stop for the fare.

Once the nuns had to pick me up from a police station, and they pretended to be really concerned and kind towards me in front of the police officers but as soon as we were in the car they started to batter me.

I had contracted scabies and as soon as we arrived back at Croome Court the nuns would shave my head and put me in a bath filled with toilet disinfectant. Afterwards I had to wear my pyjamas and scrub the wooden floors with a week old water and also with added toilet disinfectant every day.

Needless to say, my pyjamas got wet and I was punished yet again for 'carelessly spoiling it'.

After this event I ran away along the railway line and somehow got the fare to flee home to my parents. I told them what had happened in Croome Court and that I would not go back there.

My father made a complaint but on 19 October 1971 the City of Coventry Council's education department wrote to a Father Manion of Besford Court Residential School, which is, where Croome Court was based, stating that 'it would be in Rafael's best interests to remain at your school.' This was written by TJ Bond, the assistant director of education of the Council.

My parents were shocked and my father wrote to the nuns and asked for a meeting. My father tried to keep me home but they threatened him with prison, should he go against the Home Office care order.

When my father told me this I grabbed 21 of my father's valium tablets that he took for his TB, and ran to a friend's house and swallowed the pill to take my own life. My friend saw me collapsing and instantly called an ambulance.

When I woke up in hospital and realised that I was still alive I got extremely upset and aggressive, as I wanted it all to be over and die. The suicide attempt is recorded in my care records as well.

The nurses would not believe me, when I said that I had tried to kill myself because I was abused by the nuns, and refused to listen to anything I tried to say about it. They sided with the Sisters.

The psychiatrist in the hospital later wrote in his report that I obviously tried to commit suicide due to my horrendous experiences in Croome Court and that I should not be sent back there. He was the only one showing some compassion and understanding but to no avail, as this was sadly ignored by Social Services and I was sent back straight away until 1972.

Then, the Education Department released me back home. I was sent to St Ann's School again for the remainder of the term.

I ran away several times more from the violence and unspeakable abuse of the Sisters of Charity of St Paul the Apostle but to no avail, it only made things worse, as you can imagine. Nobody but my father and mother believed me. The social workers, police, nurses at the hospital and the doctors, all fell for the pathetic show of fake compassion that the nuns displayed in front of witnesses.

My father tried to get me out of Croome Court again but he was threatened with legal action should he try to keep me home, as I was still under the care order of Croome Court.

On one occasion a certain assistant director of education at the local council wrote to Father Manion: 'It would be in Rafael's best interest to remain in your school' [Croome Court]. This was devastating to my father and me.

When I returned to Croome Court I went back to the dormitory and told the boys there that I would not be staying there but would simply run away again. About five or six other boys wanted to come with me; one of them was called Colin.

We all went downstairs, and saw the nuns come up the driveway, and we quickly hid underneath the kitchen tables. The nuns came into the kitchen and caught us. They knew that I was the ringleader and they instantly separated me from the others.

They started beating me and pulling my hair. Then they stripped me naked and ripped my clothes off me and took all the boys into one room. The nuns grabbed one lad and started whipping him with a long leather strap on his backside. Every boy started instantly screaming, when they were hit as well.

When they got hold of me again, and held me down they whipped me also with the leather strap but I was trying my best not to cry. This made them even angrier and they went into a frenzy, even competing with each other, each grabbing the strap from the other in a fight to hit me.

The nuns then put me back into a cupboard again, and were saying horrible things to me, like: 'You are the devil.' When they put me into the cupboard I was completely naked, and they locked me in for the whole day. It was pitch black inside and I had no idea what time of the day it was, or what was happening. It was absolutely horrifying.

Another time, on an open day in Croome Court, a priest, who turned out to be the Archbishop of Birmingham, George Dwyer, visited and we started to chat about his vintage car that bore the same initials as my name.

In the conversation, I blew the whistle to the archbishop and told him that the Sisters would beat me up all the time, and hit me with straps. His answer was simply: 'Oh, the nuns wouldn't do that! They are nice people!' He, too, just like the other persons of authority, refused to believe me.

You might imagine, how that made me feel and influence for a long time - knowing that the nuns as people that hold power over children's lives and future could abuse their authority and our trust to get away even with organised abuse, other crimes and even murder, without ever being held accountable for it.

At least, ultimately, my suicide attempt had been the ticket for my leaving Croome Court, as the Sisters of Charity of St Paul the Apostle must have realised that I was a too big a liability to them in the long run, especially, as they were unable despite all their violent efforts to silence me or to break my spirit.

They knew that I would try to run away again and to tell people outside about their secret abuse and ongoings. Eventually I was at last moved to another institution from there, to Father Hudson's Home in Coleshill.

Chapter 6:

The Time without Memory -
Father Hudson's Home and St Edward's
Boys Home in Coleshill:

This chapter is a particularly strange one, as I cannot recall any details of the time in the Father Hudson's Home except for having been found by police, when I tried to run away from there. I was at Father Hudson's home in Coleshill for about four months.

It seems very strange indeed that I can recall almost every single detail of all the other places, or better: hell holes, and the people who abused me and the other survivors. How can it be that I have a total memory gap of this home, and my mind goes totally blank?!

Father Hudson's Society is the Social Care Agency of the Archdiocese of Birmingham. In my understanding the Father Hudson Society has not operated residential homes since 1984 but is still currently running a range of services including adoption, fostering, residential and day care for older people and those with disabilities, which I find very worrying.

I tried to obtain my records from Father Hudson's Society but they claim they could not find any records from my time there. Some priests of this home were later convicted as abusers.

I ran away on one occasion from there but was picked up by police at Flechemsted. They arrested me but brought me to my father's home and told my parents that I had been caught truant.

My sister was also put into a care home, where it later turned out that the children had been subjected to drugs and abuse and illegal mind experimentation. I strongly suspect that Father Hudson's home was being used in the same way - as a kind of experimental facility.

Russia was scouting for gifted children, removed them from their parents and sent them to secret intelligence schools to train them as spies or for various intelligence gathering specialties and for this the Russian secret service had a system of coding the children as 'retarded', 'linguistically disadvantaged', when in fact they were intelligent, multilingual and from various mixed ethnic backgrounds. So the West started to do the same, and what better partner in crime than the Vatican and Anglican international network!

In this way the residential care homes run by nuns and monks received funding from the Home Office via social services placements and often made extra income by subjecting the children to secret test programmes and to enforced adoption schemes without telling any third parties, and certainly not our parents, about it.

After all, the times were paranoid with the Cold War ongoing and mind experiments were done by the Russians and as a response by the CIA and other secret Western agencies and military facilities that collaborated with religious orders on a special deal of deniability with the Vatican, as they needed a constant supply of especially chosen children, who were labelled in codes, for their various experiments.

A man called Sidney Gottlieb got a Western world carte blanche and licence to kill by the CIA and others, which he used to establish torture facilities all over Europe and in the United States. His main laboratory, filled with poisons, toxins, and drugs from all over the world, including the most exotic ones, was in Fort Dietrich.

He had no supervisor, as the CIA and their partners didn't want to be liable for his mass murders, and acted with deniability. Nobody knew who he was and how he looked. All people knew was that he had a reputation of being mild-mannered.

He recruited former Nazi doctors for his experiments, who used their experience from the concentration camps for his 'tests'. He had subjected children and adults in all sorts of facilities to a wide range of drugs, and tortured them with them. He also had them sedated, then revived them into a state of hyperactivity, just to have them exposed to electroshocks.

Numerous anonymous mass graves were his legacy all over the surroundings of his 'facilities', including Catholic residential children's homes, like the ones I was placed in.

Think about it: We were all isolated from our families or even orphans. We were described as 'retarded' and 'poor in English' - but it was often used as a code of opposites by the religious orders, under whose care we were officially placed, for 'clever', 'multicultural', 'multi-lingual-, 'intelligent', 'inquisitive', and we were abused, so that the human spirit was driven out of us.

In many warring countries these tactics are used to train sleepers for possible future attacks on other nations, or for espionage and could be done in deniability.

Much has been covered in the press over time but the deeper hidden agenda of these places and the shielding of the Church through the intelligence agencies is still ongoing. I strongly suspect that the IICSA was very much instructed not to investigate into the facilities I was at because of their secret government involvement.

I attended this school for a year but often played truant because I knew I did not belong there and was underchallenged and deprived of a real education that I was craving.

As part of peer pressure and trying to fit in with the neighbourhood boys I was caught shoplifting and I was placed in the care of Coventry Council by the Coventry Juvenile Court in January 1973, at the age of thirteen. They sent me to a Remand Centre near Leicester for a few weeks, which was a very violent institution.

I was hit and beaten up by both the staff and the older boys. It was an evil place. We had to sleep in a big dormitory, just like in the other facilities. At night I could hear boys screaming and on more than one occasion I heard, how a boy was being raped.

I think the older boys, who were about 15 or 16, were sexually abusing younger boys in the room. I kept my head under my covers and did not look up, as I was too afraid that they might pick me next. I believe that the staff knew what was going on but they did nothing to protect the vulnerable children.

I was then moved to the notorious Tennal Assessment Centre.

Chapter 7:

The Paedophile Gang Hotspot - The Tennal Assessment Centre, Birmingham

I was sent to the Tennal Assessment Centre in Birmingham for four months, when I was still 13. This centre was later exposed as one of the most prolific child abuser institutions, with so-called pillars of society involved in the rape and torture of children. There were several serial abusers, who were successfully prosecuted and convicted after Operation Camassia by West Midlands Police.

Their names are: Robert Glover, Arthur Birch, Terry Goodall, Peter Brook and Eugene Devotti. Almost 100 individuals brought forward claims for abuse against these men and Birmingham City Council. The sad thing is that in this matter we older survivors were deprived of justice, as there were statutory limitations applied.

I was abused by Eugene Devotti, who was besides being the night duty manager at the Tennal Assessment Centre and also the organist at St Chad's Cathedral. One can see the close links between the council, the social workers and the church, which are often present in most child abuse prone facilities, as it is about organised criminality.

There were hundreds of victims coming forward in various police investigations as well but to my knowledge only 60 went to court. During my stay there 28 boys I knew were running away in one month alone!

Everything at the Tennal Assessment Centre evolved around cigarettes, which were treated like a currency. Some of the staff paid the boys with cigarettes for sexual abuse.

In the dormitory the older boys pressured me to perform a sex act on Eugene Devotti, who was a teacher, night manager but also the Cathedral organist in exchange for cigarettes. I went to Devotti's office and he took his penis out. Neither of us talked. I knew what he expected of me and I performed the act on him.

Afterwards he gave me seven or eight cigarettes and I felt unspeakably ashamed and disgusted. I never ever did this again. I didn't know his name back then but was told years later by the police that he was called Eugene Devotti and that he was also organist at St Chad's cathedral. He was later jailed for eight years at the age of 79. Late justice at least for some survivors of his evil.

Once I think somebody also tried to interfere with me in my deep sleep. I woke up suddenly, with my pyjama bottoms down and my genitalia exposed. I was feeling hazy and still half-asleep, when somebody was standing over me.

Rape was also common amongst the boys in the Tennal Assessment Centre. The older boys seemed to jump in and out of the younger boys' beds. It was one of the most horrific places I have been to.

60 survivors of the Tennal Assessment Centre went to court to sue Birmingham Council in 2001 and next to Eugene Devotti, also Arthur Birch and Tony Goodhall were jailed for eight years.

The Tennal Assessment Centre abuse is particularly significant, as almost all of the staff were in on the abuse and cover ups and made sure that even the police wouldn't listen to our pleas for help. It never occurred to Birmingham Council to even wonder why so many boys regularly tried to escape from there.

Imagine, you are being abused by a person of trust and authority, who is being protected also by the other staff, who are supposed to care for you and give you a good education! Instead you learn that you cannot trust anybody with authority, as they are more likely than not abusers and part of a wider network.

In my experience of the various institutions I have been admitted to and placed against my will and that of my parents, they have all been part of the huge Vatican abuse, trafficking and illegal or secret human experimentation chain.

It is no accident that files are being sealed and the churches and Home Office are desperate to avoid any court cases, as then they would be forced to present documents. Hence an army of double agent lawyers is being briefed to try to reach out of court settlements via NDAs and to delay any process of justice for as long as possible.

In many cases the statutes of limitations had already run out, and where they were still valid, the church tried to buy time via PR stunts, fake apologies and by setting up bogus charities that had the only aim to trap the survivors in yet another way of silencing them.

Charities have also been set up that were survivor support smokescreens, like telephone helplines that only referred the survivors cynically back to the abuser organisation, namely the church, Home Office and to the diocese that was responsible for the institutions at the time.

These charities often are simply intelligence gathering entities on behalf of the Vatican and Anglican One Church that suggest that safeguarding and survivors support is now in place but it couldn't be further from the truth.

The next institution I was placed in was the notorious St Gilbert's, when I was fourteen.

Chapter 8:

Sealing its documents is in itself revealing - St Gilbert's Approved School in Worcestershire

I was sent to St Gilbert's Approved School in Worcestershire at the age of thirteen. The school was run by the now notorious child abusers also known as Christian Brothers or as the Catholic Order the De La Salle Brothers.

My first impression of St Gilbert's was that it was okay. The other boys there seemed friendly. I was mainly doing carpentry work at first, repairing parts of the school. There were no other classes other than woodwork. We were all expected to maintain the building of the school.

They were self-sufficient also as a farm, keeping their own livestock and some of the 150 boys were expected to help out everywhere in the running of the farm, too.

For decades, thirty years to be precise, there was a campaign to unravel and expose the truth about the sadistic abuse and rape that the Brothers could unhinderedly commit without being held accountable.

Parents, who had complained, were ignored, boys, who had turned even to the police in their despair were also ignored and not believed and no investigations initiated for a long time.

The Christian De La Salle Brothers humiliated and degraded the boys through all sorts of abuse, including force feeding them their own vomit. Others were raped and molested in many unspeakable ways, others were beaten until they were black and blue all over their bodies.

As the boys were viewed as 'delinquent' the De La Salle Brothers saw their classification as a carte blanche to torture the boys as they pleased. They were usually between 11 and 15 years young, and were sent there for petty theft or vandalism.

The De La Salle Brothers were paid for providing the boys with a good education and to straighten them out, teaching them right from wrong. But what the boys were experiencing was violence and sadism and abuse in every shape and size.

The police and even the Home Office protected the Christian Brothers, when parents complained officially. It is only since 2014 that West Mercia Police opened an investigation into the historic child abuse at St Gilbert's.

Some of the De La Salle Brothers turned out to be also officially charged with rape and other child abuse, some were even reallowed as teachers after their sentences were fulfilled.

Some documents however are still sealed until 2044. This might be to do with the secret involvement of the Christian Brothers with illegal and classified experimentation on the boys, which was often done by Catholic and Anglican Orders, who thus also operated under the protection and immunity of secret agencies, the military and the Vatican or Anglican Church.

For me personally the abuse in St Gilbert's was not quite as bad as it had been in Croome Court. Having said that - once a certain Brother Dominic started to approach me in a sexual manner and I resisted, as I knew the signs instantly.

I was coming back one night from a table tennis match, as I was in the team, and I went to the woodworking yard to do some work. I went into the kitchen by the yard, at about 9 or 10 pm at night, with most other boys already in the dormitory.

I was looking for food, as sometimes food was left lying around. There were onions, cabbages and other vegetables, and I was eating some of that and then went back towards the dormitory. There was an office as I went upstairs with Brother Dominic in.

He brought me into his office and started shouting at me, asking why I was out of bed. He then started caressing my arm in an obviously sexual manner, and stroking me. I knew immediately what was going on and realised that it was his way of grooming me.

He then turned on me in rage, when I pushed him away and he started shouting at me and hit me so hard in the solar plexus that I almost fainted and couldn't breathe. I was only a very small boy and Brother Dominic was a very big man.

Another time Brother Dominic came into the table tennis room and knocked me to the ground and stamped repeatedly on me. There was no warning whatsoever. I was simply dazed and numb and confused. The other boys witnessed this but didn't dare to utter a sound or do anything.

I was also severely battered by Mr Wareing and Mr Holby on various occasions. For example, Mr Wareing, who was also a very big man, would grab my ear and use it to twist my whole body onto the floor.

Mr Wareing, who was the gym teacher, would call me an 'idiot' and a 'divvy', when I kicked the ball against the gym wall, and missed the target. In the game we were playing we could only score an even number and I had said an odd number.

He would then call me names and rub his feet into my face, when I said something back to him. He would beat me up many times in the gym. He punched me onto the floor, and then slapped and kicked me in front of the other boys. He did this frequently and he was feared for his 'specialty' throughout the school.

After all these years, I came to think that abuse is a normal way of life and part of education, as I didn't know it any different.

On another occasion, I kept seeing Mr Wareing staring at me in the dining hall. When I got up to leave the dining hall, he called me over. I went over to his table and he then hit me, and told me that I had to 'Start eating properly!' I had no idea what he meant or what I had done wrong but it seemed like he simply had it in for me.

The man who was in charge of the Tuck shop would also often call us boys over, and then use his knee to give us a 'dead leg' on our thighs. I would almost always have a bruise on my right-hand side thigh.

Mr Holby, whose nickname was 'Piggy' would sometimes call boys over to him, and he would then grab us by our ears and use them to twist us onto the ground, and he would then call me names and rub his feet also in my face. He was known and feared for this across the school.

It was then, when I started self-harming, cutting my arms with broken glass. I don't think that anybody was aware of it or would even care that I did. I still have scars from that time on my arms.

As a result of all this abuse I would often go to the woodwork shop and put my head in a tin of glue. Mr Selby was aware that I was sniffing glue, and persuaded me not to do it because it was bad for me.

He was one of the better teachers there, but it did not stop me from doing it. I would occasionally sniff glue in the woodwork shop for about a year, just to try and get away from the pain of being there and to cope with all the anxiety and violence.

In September 2018 two of the Christian Brothers monks were on trial for multiple charges of physical and sexual abuse at St Gilbert's. I believe one was called Brother Wilfred but I can't remember much about him from my time there.

The abuse has left me with a complex trauma that had and has a huge impact on my life - physically, mentally, psychologically and emotionally, and it also affects my family. I only told my children about my childhood abuse ten years ago.

Until then I carried it all inside me without telling a single soul about it. Needless to say that the abuse also affects your trust in people, as the broken trust by adults sticks with you for life.

It is important to share with others and to expose the evil that has happened to us survivors, as there are very common patterns emerging and lessons to be learned worldwide.

It is vital also to remember that I was abused and sent into abusive residential schools and institutions for no other reason than I was a boy from a multicultural, multi-lingual and poor family. I was in fact a bright and inquisitive boy and a quick study, who happened to speak in a thick local Glaswegian accent in England.

I was deprived of six vital years of my childhood. The social workers, nuns, priests, teachers, who chose me for these institutions did so because of my qualities that they coded as the opposite - as 'retarded', 'under challenged', 'deprived'.

Remember, it was the time of the Cold War, and the Vatican and Anglican Church were very much used by Western governments as talent scouts and soldier material for possible wars and thus the churches were the ideal suppliers for boys with multi-lingual skills, multicultural backgrounds and with an inquisitive mind, who happened to come from poor backgrounds, so that they could be easily isolated from their parents.

This is probably one of the reasons, why documents relating not just to St Gilbert's but also to other institutions, where I was exposed to torture and mind warfare and drugs experiments, are still under seal until 2044, and why the IICSA was limiting its investigations and left exactly those institutions out.

After I left St Gilbert's I went to Bishop Ullathorne School. My father had just died and so Social Services reevaluated the situation, and decided that it was okay for me to return home to my mother and siblings.

I attended Bishop Ullathorne School for about four or five months until I turned 16. It was a comprehensive school, and it was the school of my choice, to which I should have been sent to, when I left St Ann's Primary School.

It was a fantastic time there, as I fitted in. Sadly though, for the exams I arrived too late and thus could not sit them. When I left Bishop Ullathorne School I had no formal qualifications at all.

The first job I had after school was in Coventry collier. I had to pass a number of written exams in things like health and safety, in order to become a miner. I passed all the entry exams without any problems, and I would have hardly achieved this, had I been truly retarded.

The Council has let me and numerous other children down badly. I passed those vocational exams with ease, whilst many others failed them.

Chapter 9:

The Fake Apologies without Consequence - May we introduce: The League of the professional Vatican Liars

At the time, when I was contacted and later visited by two high ranking leaders of the Roman Catholic Church to hear my case: Archbishop Bernard Longley from the Archdiocese of Birmingham and the Papal Nuncio from the Vatican, Archbishop Claudio Gugerotti, I was still hoping for justice through the church.

A visit by the Archbishop of Birmingham, Bernard Longley - another Judas who sealed his fake apology and broken promise of help in my house with a cup of my own coffee, © Rafael Viola

I welcomed the opportunity to get heard and to build bridges, albeit fragile ones. How naive I was to think the Roman Catholic Church was really interested in bringing justice for survivors and that they truly repented, as they should have done! After all, that is, what they tell the public to do.

Archbishop Bernard Longley insisted on visiting me in my house for a cup of coffee. All he did in the end was use the visit as his PR stunt and as an opportunity to patronise me and only offer me his prayer. He was not repentant at all and his predecessor, Cardinal Nichols, never even made an effort of reconciliation with the survivors, never mind showing remorse.

ARCHDIOCESE OF BIRMINGHAM

Telephone: (0121) 236 9090
Fax: (0121) 212 0171
E-Mail: archbishop@rc-birmingham.org

ARCHBISHOP'S HOUSE
8 SHADWELL STREET
BIRMINGHAM
B4 6EY

Mr Rafael Viola
136 College Street
Hill Top
Nuneaton
Warwickshire
CV10 7BJ

3 August 2019

Dear Mr Viola

I am very grateful to you for so kindly welcoming me to your home in Nuneaton when I came to visit you with Mr Andrew Haley on 30 July 2019. Please thank your daughter for thoughtfully providing us with a cup of coffee together and for supporting you in preparation for the visit.

I was very interested to learn about your family's connections with some of the local Catholic schools and to have an insight into your own early experiences growing up in a Catholic family. I also wish to thank you for sharing with me so many other elements of your life story and for showing me how the terrible experiences of your childhood have had a lasting and negative impact on your life.

I apologise unreservedly to you, on behalf of the Archdiocese of Birmingham, for the harm done to you at Croome Court School. I realise from our conversation the great burden that this has been to you over the years, as well as to those who are close to you, and I also apologise to you for this. I recognise with profound regret the failure to provide you with support and compensation at an earlier date.

I want to assure you that I am actively pursuing a way for the trustees of the Archdiocese to meet your claim for compensation without reference to the legal limitation that previously prevented claimants from receiving compensation from the Church. I hope to be able to give you further news about this before very long.

1/continued

Mr Rafael Viola

I have recently had individual meetings with other survivors of abuse at Croome Court School so that I could also apologise to them and seek to redress the harm caused to them. This includes actively exploring the possibility of offering compensation to them.

I hope that this helps to show that the Archdiocese wishes to change its approach to survivors of abuse, and to show them the compassion and understanding that they deserve. Listening to you has helped me understand better what we need to do and I am very grateful to you for teaching me this important lesson.

Andrew Haley and I promised that we would look into some practical ways of assisting you, in particular in relation to your healthcare needs and in applying for statutory benefits. We will give this issue some further thought before contacting you again.

May I finally ask you to forgive me and the Catholic Church for the harm that was done to you under the cloak of religion? I know that I have no right to expect such forgiveness, but I feel that you have had the right to be asked this for a long time and I am sorry that it is only now that I do so. I hope that this letter may go some way towards healing the abiding harm that you have suffered over so many years.

Once again, I thank you for meeting with us at your home in Nuneaton. I promise to remember you, together with your family, in my prayers.

With every kind wish.

Yours sincerely in Christ

+Bernard Longley
Archbishop of Birmingham

Cc: Andrew Haley (Diocesan Head of Safeguarding Transformation)
       David Brooks (Diocesan Chief Operating Officer)

29/10/2015

Archbishop's House
Birmingham

To Mr. Rafael Viola

May Our Lord Jesus Christ
go before you to guide you,
behind you to guard you,
above you to defend you,
beside you to support you,
within you to strengthen you.
May the prayers of this Mother
lighten your burden and guide
your footsteps in the way of peace.

+ Bernard Longley
Archbishop of Birmingham

Mary, Mother of God *(tapestry – Turvey)*

Abacus (Colour Printers) Ltd., Cumbria. (01229) 885361

Another liar and Judas Brother faking it! Meet the then Papal Nuncio Claudio Gugerotti, who also promised an apology from Pope Francis, for which I am still waiting three years later! © Rafael Viola

On the contrary, Cardinal Nichols used every opportunity to worm himself out of any responsibility with lame excuses, saying the vast system of religious orders and institutions made it impossible for a cardinal to oversee and enforce any enduring preventative safeguarding regulation.

At the IICSA inquiry he sent in a sick note quoting migraines, and did not even show up. He and the Archbishop of Canterbury, Justin Welby, have promised to enforce a safeguarding policy in their ONE CHURCH agreement, which is a total farce, as all they have done is regrouping the old facilitators of CSA and child trafficking and other organised church criminality with their own high finance company via Church House in Westminster, and placed them strategically in CoE and RCC parishes in positions as churchwardens, PCC members, Sunday School teachers, safeguarding officers, data officers, legal and financial advisors etc.

All the fake apologies by high ranking church leaders, from popes to bishops, amount to nothing but mockery of the survivors and have no consequence except for the effect on survivors that the churches cannot be trusted at all.

The night before the Archbishop of Birmingham's visit, my lawyer, who later turned out to be a double agent, as he tried to persuade me to sign a non-disclosure agreement, turned up on my doorstep and asked for my daughter to meet him later in his hotel to bring him documents he claimed he needed to see to influence her.

I was outraged and told another lawyer about this, who said that he would not do or say anything to discredit a colleague.

When Archbishop Bernard Longley came to see me in my humble home on 30 July 2019 I had to borrow two chairs, so that he and his colleague would have somewhere to sit, as my living room is taken up by my hospital bed. I have been very ill for a long time now and can no longer walk.

We had a very long meeting with the Archbishop. He mainly listened carefully to my story and to my experiences and suggestions as to what lessons can be learned from this process of seeking justice.

Archbishop Longley accepted my account of events and told me that he felt a deep sense of shame. He told me that he wanted to apologise to me on behalf of the whole Catholic Church. Again, I trusted the empty words of a person of church authority, who later never followed up on them in action.

I was played yet again with just another PR stunt and silencing instrument - this time a personal visit. I can only imagine that the archdiocese was already so much under attack by the public that the Archbishop had to at least be seen keen on resolving the issue of historical abuse.

My exposing publicly the abuse in their various institutions and my intentions to take the Catholic Church to court was alerting the Archbishop enough to try to silence me through flattery and in a civil manner, faking his repentance.

The Institute for Criminology and Justice Report showed that the use of as double agents acting lawyers before a visit by a high ranking church figure is quite a common strategy to try to impress or even set the mood for the importance of the meeting in the survivor, so that they would be more inclined to sign the NDA.

The lawyers then would secretly try to gather as much material and as many informal statements from the survivors and their families to use against them and to discredit all the witnesses involved, even the wider or deceased family.

If they could not find anything on behalf of their secret client, the Church, they would simply invent lies and feed them back to their paymaster.

Chapter 10:

Trials and Tribulations

It is interesting how the memory works. Much has been researched and written about losing one's memory after a trauma. Or how survivors often take decades to even remember any traumatic event or for a memory to resurface.

When it does, it might come in a surprisingly quiet way but often happens unexpectedly also like a lightning bolt. It might start with a dream or with an image popping up in one's mind. It hits you with all its force. There might even be a wave or a fully unleashed flood of memories forcing their way into the conscience out of the subconscious mind.

It probably happens, when we are at last ready to remember and have developed mechanisms to cope with it. Why else would it happen so often, when we have started the process of going back to the roots of our trauma to seek justice and recognition of the truth?!

From my experience many survivors do not even have access to therapy or are too sceptical and suspicious of the various offers that I have for example received from various double agent Catholic charities that are mostly suggested to us via the mediators of the dioceses.

Whom you can trust in this labyrinth of the churches' hamster wheel schemes is an art of survival itself! The churches all want to buy time, if they can no longer deny any liability, and hope that the survivors of historic abuse will die before the statutes of limitations, if any, run out.

It is a cynical and dishonest way of fake reconciliation that sends us survivors in circles, every time getting up our hopes of justice, when the next higher church official invites himself to a meeting with a survivor.

In my case, the Vatican must have been extremely worried that I would aim at going to court, which they naturally wanted to avoid, as I was abused in more than four of their most notorious institutions, and not all statutes of limitations had run out yet.

The Archbishop of Birmingham, Bernard Longley, and even the Papal Nuncio, Claudio Gugerotti, asked to meet me in person to do their PR stunts and try some image damage limitation. I can't believe that I even fell for their fake piety and that they still had nothing more to offer than a prayer and a handshake.

It was also no accident that they used the survivors' lawyers before the high visit to offer a NDA and to try to discredit the survivors with all means available to them, including Omerta style tactics.

Too often has our trust been violated and personal data and experiences purposefully and strategically used against us, as was the case also with so-called expert witnesses like psychiatrists, who were hired by the churches to give their 'expertise' about us.

In my case the psychiatrist in question assessed my whole history and that of my family after only a brief meeting, for which I had waited months, and he got it totally wrong. So much so that I had a lawyer respond to the Professor's every single misrepresentation in his statements.

He was clearly operating on behalf of the RCC and applying Nazi methodology and vocabulary, which retraumatized not just me but also my whole family.

He and the army of experts is part of a very dark and sinister force within the RCC that saw the Vatican collaborating already during and after

WWII with former Nazi scientists and doctors, who had developed even more intrusive and unsupervised tests on people, including us children, in various government projects and international as well as national secret agencies, like the Western world CIA experiments of Sydney Gottlieb and others.

Gottlieb and his cohorts had a worldwide licence to kill and to discard their dead bodies literally in mass graves without ever being held responsible for torture and crimes against humanity, as all Western governments gave them carte blanche, including the United Kingdom.

As we know now, the Vatican had its own equally radical and unethical illegal human experimentation programmes, for which the religious orders were also paid.

No surprise then, that the exact institutions I was a resident and survivor of were left out of the IICSA inquiry, as many files are inaccessible under classified categories and can only be opened in some twenty more years.

Chapter 11:

IICSA

When the IICSA began their inquiry and asked all of us survivors to attend to be heard, I believed this could have been the start of transforming historical child abuse claims in a positive way.

How wrong I was!

Imagine:

You arrive full of hope and anticipation in the hotel the night before the IICSA is about to start. There I am meeting with four other survivors of Croome Court, who are also there to present their testimony, and we share the same lawyers.

I could see in their faces that something was feeling off - one of the witnesses, who was represented by a different lawyer from ours, had a bombshell for us:

Jane Jones, the long-time social worker and safeguarding coordinator of the Archdiocese of Birmingham, who was supposed to testify at the IICSA the next day, had just tendered her resignation.

This news hit us in shock, and we immediately sat down to discuss how to proceed without her. The Birmingham Archdiocese was the only one in fact that refused to pass on any names of abusers to the Catholic Safeguarding Organisation but Jane Jones claimed that she always passed on the names of perpetrators to the authorities and police for investigation.

Jane Jones did show up for her testimony but she played on lack of memory and indeed, could not even state her own name. It smelt of a dead fish tactical sabotage approach by the Birmingham Archdiocese because she obviously timed her resignation conveniently for the Archdiocese on Friday before the Inquiry started on the Monday.

The IICSA later concluded that Jane Jones 'did not modernise the safeguarding team and manage her numerous responsibilities effectively.' The Charity Commission announced in 2019 that it would open a statutory inquiry into the Archdiocese of Birmingham, as it showed disparities between the Archdiocese's audits and those of CSAS like record keeping.

Records were not kept in compliance and the problems were not really addressed until then and responses were inadequate.

We entered the courtroom as a group, and took the atmosphere in:

The crowds are gathering in the public gallery of the courtroom. Some of them are survivors, who have waited almost all their lives for this moment.

They are full of hope and silent victory and triumph in expectation of the final verdict of the jury. Will the time of trauma and retraumatization, the endless worries, anxieties, if not the pain that they endured physically and psychologically, be at last over? The boulders fall off their shoulders?

Many have endured more than a human being should ever have to endure - not just the initial abuse and trauma but also the consequences they had on their whole lives.

They lost their jobs, their livelihood, their families and friends, when they spoke out or couldn't cope with their suffering in silence any longer.

Some fell into the traps of artificial comfort via alcohol or drugs, only to experience that they fell into an ever deeper and darker abyss of abuse.

Many are thinking also and especially of those, who haven't made it to this day and succumbed to despair and pressure or sickness but there are also those, who had turned their lives around and drew renewed strength from all the struggles and refused to let themselves get knocked down yet again by the churches, who abused them in such horrible ways over and again.

They are now all the richer in experience and in friendships that they made along the way.

And they pass on their knowledge and memories to help others. All of these emotions and memories are silently but with loud heartbeats filling the atmosphere of the courtroom.

Then there are those, who come out of curiosity, even a bit of shame that they did not speak out, when they should have done and even doubted the survivors and fought them all the way to this day.

They are now suddenly sitting with their heads bowed and looking in a new sense of humility at the survivors in anticipation of the judgement to come. They know it will also be a judgement on their behaviour and lack of willingness to help and support those, who had needed and asked for it.

A cramped room filled with clergy, cardinals, and arch/bishops in their cassocks and ceremonial gear with their army of Savile Row tailor suited lawyers on one side, chatting away with each other, hugging and kissing each other, exchanging the latest news and gossip and strategies.

On the other side but in the same space we survivors were seated. The church representatives blanked us completely and thus put us literally and psychologically into 'our place', only giving us the strategic dirty look with utmost arrogance and contempt, out to intimidate us.

Otherwise, they totally ignored us. Not one of the officials came over to any of us and had a kind word or an apology or at least an encouraging smile for us.

In the inquiry room I was seated amongst 30+ members of the Catholic clergy from Bishops to Nuns to Monseigneurs which was already emotionally very triggering.

Jane Jones couldn't remember 'anything'. On the next day Cardinal Nichols, the former Archbishop of Birmingham and present Cardinal in Westminster Cathedral, was due to appear but the same co-participant, who had told us about the resignation of Jane Jones informed us now that Nichols had handed in a mysterious sick note quoting 'migraine' twelve hours before having to make his appearance.

So the only person who didn't attend and who should have attended was Cardinal Nichols. I listened to the read out statements of apology and proposals for change for four out of the five days, with my patience and expectations and hopes turning increasingly into frustration and anger at the unfolding farce the IICSA sessions turned out to be.

Another day of frustration and disappointment and growing anger for us survivors.

On the third day of the inquiry, we were told that the panel had read statements from the survivors but was unable to read them out in full at the inquiry due to time. For years I and the other survivors had prepared for our statements, had countless conversations, meetings, and gave testimony that was legally binding.

I was told that my statement would be read out in full. Instead a brief 2 minute summary was read aloud that did not even cover the basics. This enraged not just me. We were all invited on the pretence that it would be beneficial for our healing and that our voices were going to be heard in the inquiry. Now we were silenced yet again.

To appease me they agreed they would read my story out to the public. On day 4 they did do this, but in this insulting joke of a brief summary which lasted only 2 minutes. The Archbishop of Birmingham, Bernard Longley, was sitting in the dock, waiting to be sworn in, whilst I read my two minute statement out.

Suddenly I was told to stop and I protested, as I had not even finished. My lawyer told me to be silent but I wouldn't do as I was told but called the IICSA a farce and a joke.

I screamed at my lawyer in disgust and whilst my brother was wheeling me out of the courtroom I was still shocked at their audacity to treat me and other survivors like this.

I protested at one point on my way out to Professor Jay - after being completely ignored by her - and to the panel about how disgusting it was, and that the inquiry was already turning out to be a corrupt farce.

I left that building protesting with anger. The treatment at the hands of the IICSA hit me extremely hard and retraumatised me, and resulted in me having a mental breakdown and an angina attack and I had to be admitted to St Thomas Hospital for the night.

Not one person from the inquiry showed me or other survivors any empathy, compassion, or concern, so on the fifth day I simply left; I had heard enough of the farcical show they were conducting, and decided to no longer have a part in this alibi appearance.

Later I was contacted by various survivors, who had been present at the IICSA and who were also ignored and not heard with their statements, like Joanna Brittain, who wanted to testify against Sherbourne boarding school.

They were all lied to and not given a chance to tell their stories. There are numerous survivors, who came to the IICSA at their own cost, like Joanna and me, and many others, and we would get no compensation for the tickets and accommodation costs.

I shared my own hotel room with a co-participant, who had been badly retraumatized like the rest of us and I bought food and drinks for him, and paid also for his breakfast the next morning. The IICSA paid lawyers and clergy their fees and costs but yet we survivors were left to our own devices.

The fellow survivor I had taken under my wings was told by his lawyer when he asked whether he could pay him some of the expenses that his 'law firm was not a travel agency'! What an insult and disregard for human dignity!

No one has approached me since the inquiry and there were so many other participants there that day who also were never heard. We were all misled to believe we were going to be heard and to give evidence. This was so far from the truth. If anything, it was more trauma and disappointment added to our load.

I left after that and took a taxi to Euston Station and went back home on the train. These are my memories of the IICSA.

I only heard from the IICSA again, when they contacted my lawyer about me using my real name on social media. They asked me to remove the blogs, where my story was told. They also wanted me to use my code name/number in any further future interviews and publications.

It is interesting to note that all the various institutions I was abused at were left out of the IICSA inquiry. Many files are classified and sealed until after 2044. I have been later told by the Christian Brothers of the De La Salle Order that they do not feel responsible for my abuse, as they were employees of the Home Office and that I should therefore contact the Home Office for compensation instead.

The IICSA did not even contact me personally but only my daughter and my lawyer, which was outrageous, too.

This was shortly before the Final Report was due, and I can only assume that they were very nervous being presented as hostile, selective and manipulative towards the survivors, using the demand for removing the blog as a pressurising tool to silence me and other survivors with their publications and prevent us all from speaking out publicly against the shortcomings and serious failings of the inquiry.

The IICSA then suddenly, after all this time of no contact, did offer at last emotional support and legal advisors but their short list of therapists and lawyers was clearly biassed, as they were from the context of the very abuser organisation, the Roman Catholic Church, or had at least clear connections to the church.

The charities I had been given turned out also to be cul-de-sacs. In one case scenario I was told after a long conversation with a charity helpline that they would only listen sympathetically but had no powers or information service and would recommend to me to contact the diocese again - thus sending me back to the very perpetrator institution, which is totally unacceptable.

It is like sending a victim of the Mafia back to the Mafia clan chief to ask for justice and compensation, and thus to have him also admit that he is the head of a crime organisation, who gave the orders and runs all spiderwebs involved facilitating their organised crimes and cover ups.

That is exactly, what the Vatican does,and is and in the U.K. they even have ultimately brought the Anglican See also on board in their One Church secretly paedophile sheltering agreement that they sell to the public as shared safeguarding policies.

If you want to protect children from abuse in the churches, you keep them at home. The churches cannot be trusted. Even the IICSA concluded this in their reports.

Chapter 12:

The Big Torment - the IICSA Aftermath

The weeks leading up to the Final Report of the IICSA were a time of retraumatizing, turmoil and upheaval in my life and of all survivors and those, who share in their concerns and fight for justice.

The constant propaganda of the churches mocked us survivors by releasing statements that Child Safeguarding measures were long in place, meaning only that the old CSA facilitators were now all the wiser and more clever and twisted the recommendations with their own implementations by putting their regrouped experienced abuse veterans into new strategic positions.

Suddenly old paedophile facilitators and child traffickers are to be found again in the same churches and institutions, now even as child protection safeguarding officers, parish secretaries, PCC members and chairs, legal advisors, and Sunday school teachers. Some even in several controlling positions and as secret handlers for the arch/bishops.

I and many other survivors felt very anxious, frustrated and without great hope left by now about this upcoming final report. Too many stones were thrown our way already during the Inquiry but especially in the last few months, when I started to become more outspoken and critical of the emerging bias of the IICSA.

But the press is now increasingly more engaging with survivors and although I am sceptical, how long their interest will last and about their true motives, social media are an invaluable tool 24/7 for connecting with other survivors worldwide and for exposing the ever same patterns of organised church crimes and especially the cover ups and Omerta culture.

The idea of memorial benches by the IICSA for raising awareness for CSA enraged every single survivor I know, as we felt even more let down by the inquiry. These kinds of benches are usually placed by families of deceased people as a place of remembering. We felt like we were being treated like the dead, and not offered concrete real help and support.

Those of us, who spoke out against the benches or asked for benches to be put on the grounds of our places of abuse were simply blocked by the consultants to the IICSA, which is outrageous in itself, as they proclaim they are acting in our interests.

Most of us are even still waiting for compensation and recognition of our suffering and we expected to see the laws changed in favour of prevention of CSA and of prosecution of historic abuse.

The Final Report of the IICSA did not even recommend the removal of statutory limitations, as was done in other international inquiries. Mandatory reporting was included but why not the former as well? It would have cost nothing to add the removal of statutory limitations to the Final Report.

Countess Sigrid von Galen had written and published my and John Lamb's story about our time in Croome Court in a blog that found a wide readership worldwide with strong responses echoing our fight for justice.

I was invited to a breakfast radio show by Sonia Poulton, which also saw great pouring out of public support. Meanwhile I also gave TV interviews to the BBC and on radio and podcast shows.

After that the IICSA let their lawyers contact my lawyer to say that I am in breach of data protection by revealing my own identity, and they forced us to take the blog down.

It was extremely distressing for me, and it seemed like sinister mockery that the IICSA offered me in the same letter and later in phone calls counselling for any support in the matter. It doesn't get any more twisted than that!

Silencing me and other survivors in this way shows that the IICSA seems to have a hidden agenda - to limit the damage to the churches.

We come back to that later again, when we look at the devil's advocates in their own chapter. The closer the time came for the final report, the more the IICSA revealed its nervousness about survivors rebelling and publicly questioning its integrity.

The Institute for Criminology and Justice looked at the strategies and processes of the churches in their own independent report after the release of the Final IICSA report.

Needless to say, for us survivors - those, who are still alive, that is - these weeks cost us again dearly in terms of health and emotional well being.

We had also been given a very selective and short list of lawyers chosen by the IICSA as suggestions for legal advisors, most of whom we meanwhile knew to be acting as double agents for both the churches and to the disadvantage of us survivors by trying to bully us into Non-disclosure agreements, so-called NDAs. Another way of silencing.

This phenomenon of double agents does also exist amongst survivors and charities - or, I should say, those, who claim to be such! It was extremely disheartening and retraumatizing as well to find out that many charities pretending to help survivors that mushroomed around the time the IICSA started and during the inquiry were and are actually hidden tentacles and spiderwebs of the churches and other perpetrator circles with a huge budget for bribery and espionage.

Charities were simply used for intelligence gathering and to manipulate and entrap survivors. Helplines were designed to simply find out where survivors were standing and what they intended to do and they were sent back to the offending institutions for further procedures, thus reabusing the abused.

Countess Sigrid von Galen has looked at the IICSA and the history of other international inquiries into child sexual abuse for the Institute for Criminology and Justice in an independent report, which I like to include in this book in parts, too.

Chapter 13:

The Anatomy of Sabotage of International Inquiries into Child Sexual Abuse, Independent ICJ Report, A Brief Summary

The Institute for Criminology and Justice:

Independent ICJ-Report into Croome Court and other Institutions:

The Anatomy of Sabotage of International Inquiries into Child Sexual Abuse

A Brief Summary

Author: Countess Sigrid von Galen

Survivors of the Catholic Church abuse, not just at Croome Court, have been failed many times by all the organisations, institutions and inquiries, including the latest of the IICSA, who were pretending to act on their behalf over decades.

The Institute for Criminology and Justice has been commissioned with an independent report based on the survivors' own experiences and testimonies with those who claimed to represent their interests in the struggle for justice.

Here is a brief summary of the independent ICJ report:

There are many common denominators of sabotage of international inquiries into child sexual abuse.

All perpetrator organisations but especially the churches, who think and plan in terms of centuries and make diocesan plans for 10 years, always play for time for as long as they get away with it.

Meanwhile they intimidate witnesses and destroy evidence to obstruct any due investigation and justice process.

Very often promises are being made that are being kept extremely vague to calm the public outcry in the hope it will simply fade away.

The churches are strategically employing PR agencies and journalists internationally to distract the public with other matters, so that readers lose their interest and focus on the abuse and other organised criminality.

The churches spend millions on their image and will use repetitive keywords like 'responsibility', 'mindfulness', 'awareness' and 'safeguarding' so often but act always contrary to their statements.

Witnesses and survivors have increasingly exchanged their experiences and shared their observations internationally, so that the systemic and organised criminality patterns and fascism of the churches became evermore transparent and visible.

The survivors describe their frustration at the arrogance and non-action and continuation of the same old patterns of the churches sheltering paedophiles and proven organised criminals amongst clergy and at the ever same legalised lawlessness that is the standard of the canon law, which the churches place higher than common or criminal law of the lands.

The Irish, Australian, British and other inquiries f.ex. were all sabotaged by the perpetrator organisations, especially the Catholic and Anglican but also other churches and wider perpetrator organisations.

The churches always try to direct and sabotage the standards of inquiries. They want to be in charge and decide who gets to investigate what and how. They will make sure that church loyal members of boards are strategically placed on all levels.

A pattern of organised criminal methodology and silencing strategy of discrediting and slandering survivors, their families and friends was emerging that was painting a picture of a perpetrator culture with far reaching tentacles and close knit local, national and international hidden associations using the means of enforcing Omerta as in organised criminality.

Survivors reported experiences of falsified so-called expert reports that were aimed at discrediting and slandering them. The experts were clearly biassed and double-agents.

Lawyers have also acted over decades worldwide as double agents, bribed by the Vatican and Anglican churches to lure survivors into NDAs and to intimidate them with threats, should they dare to speak out.

The survivors' family history was distorted to suit and justify the perpetrator organisations' institutionalised abuse and general life affecting actions.

Identities of survivors and advocates for the survivors seemed to have been leaked as insider jobs by the IICSA. The mails were sent to all recipients of the IICSA via CC! The IICSA was later fined £200.000 as penalty but the victims of these strategic attacks still await an apology, if not compensation.

Many perpetrators were only posing as survivors and set up churches near charities that were intended to lure the survivors into a false sense of security to simply gather intelligence through them and to find out what their legal intentions were.

The inquiries were often steered secretly by the churches via stakeholder groups to limit damage and to concentrate only on cases that had come out already anyway.

Needless to say that the churches set and will always set the lowest threshold, if any, for compensation and support for survivors, and again, will ensure that any compensation and help like reports, therapies and counselling or legal advice is linked to a list of their preferred candidates of experts.

Survivors present at inquiries and especially at the IICSA said that they were put into the same room as the church lawyers and high ranking officials and clergy, who intimidated them.

Apologies are offered often but almost always never being followed up with action and without any commitment to compensation.

Many survivors were forced to relive their ordeal and were retraumatised without any offer of help of counselling or looking after them also by organising accommodation.

Promises were made to the survivors with the intent never to fulfil them, only to create the impression to help the investigations, whilst documents were in fact destroyed,

The chair of the IICSA, Prof. Alexis Jay, was most likely chosen for her ability that she demonstrated already in Rotherham, to focus on a selective choice of cases that were already out in the open and to leave out those that would damage the reputation of the churches even further.

Her recommendations came also always short of real law changes, stopping short at recommending only measures that she knew could and would easily be sabotaged and ignored by the churches and other influential perpetrator circles.

In that way her reputation could stay intact and shortcomings be dismissed and represented as out of her control and blame be put on the ongoing untouchable perpetrator culture.

The cardinals and archbishops played this scenario by giving statements that the One Church had now new safeguarding procedures in place but that they were not enforceable as such everywhere, especially in religious orders.

What the likes of Justin Welby and Cardinal Nichols failed to mention though are their secret positioning of regrouped old CSA facilitators within the RCC and Anglican churches in new disguises and recycled roles as parish council secretaries, Sunday School teachers, churchwardens, legal and financial advisors and others.

They also gag their clergy and use survivor lawyers as their double agents, which has saved the churches court proceedings and the public humiliation of a bottomless pit of sexual abuse cases.

In the event of the IICSA hearings, an important witness, who had been in the employ the Birmingham Archdiocese for over 30 years resigned from her post the weekend before the Inquiry started, and pretended she had lost her memory.

More recently, two major independent board members of an inquiry in the Cologne Archdiocese also resigned before a court trial against the Cardinal of Cologne Woelki.

The churches will pretend to develop strategies that look at face value like prevention and safeguarding but which are in fact simply PR stunts.

The churches recruit and place stakeholders in a group, charity or movement as infiltrators, who can manipulate the others towards the church agenda and to sabotage any efforts and progress for truth and justice.

These double agents befriend other members and make them dependent on them, either on their opinion, financially, socially or sexually.

A more creative approach by the churches and their secret agencies moles is that of entrapping survivors in projects like book publications about or by survivors. For example, in several cases an agent posing as a survivor himself and planted by the Vatican even on an inquiry panel befriended survivors and suggested a book publication.

He invited several survivors, who had been visible and active on social media to get their voices heard in a forthcoming collection of their stories. He never ever mentioned that it would have been financed by a grant of the very Catholic charity that had tried to silence the same survivors on several occasions and tried to refer them back to the archdiocese.

Had they known that he had a contract with the charity in question they would have never agreed to contribute to this book. Needless to say in the end he outed himself in an email to say that the book would not go ahead and he named the charity in his last sentence for the first time.

This retraumatised the survivors yet again, as it became clear that he only wanted to find out where they stand and what they would reveal about their plans to expose the church even more and whether they still intended to go to court.

During all his communications with the survivors this agent disguised his persona and identity and his place of residency, typical of an undercover legend that is aimed at presenting a made up image of a broken life. He also had knowledge of the friends of the survivors, with whom they interacted on social media and tried to reach out to them, too, by using characteristics in his writing and details that they would find familiar and reminiscent.

A lot of research and surveillance must have gone into that 'project' but the agent overdid it and could be traced back to Vatican sources.

The churches have internationally employed whole armies of PR agencies, expert witnesses, lawyers, bribed prosecutors and judges, who owe them favours or are simply being blackmailed and bullied but also well paid to discredit and silence victims, whistleblowers and any witnesses.

The use of as double agents acting lawyers before a visit by a high ranking church figure is quite a common strategy to try to impress or even set the mood for the importance of the meeting in the survivor, so that the latter would be more inclined to sign the NDA.

The lawyers then would secretly try to gather as much material and as many informal statements from the survivors to use them against them and to discredit all the witnesses involved, even the wider or deceased family.

If they could not find anything on behalf of their secret client, the Church, they would try sexual advances towards family members, so that they could use that as a blackmail tool, as is often the case in the churches.

Expert witnesses, especially doctors and psychiatrists, are often paid for by the churches, and will present biassed reports, as has happened numerous times all over the world in the past as well, with survivors being presented falsely as 'uneducated, backwards, mentally disabled, immoral, addicts with a bad gene pool', which is the vocabulary of the concentration camps, where Nazi-glorified doctors experimented on incarcerated victims of all ages, and were allowed to do so even after the war with the help of the churches and sinister political forces.

As we now know, this attitude of a fake science with templates to categorise human beings is still being used to this very day, often even in many government settings under the pretence and disguise of research. It is simply a regrouping and recycling of old fascist ideology in new guises and new masks.

The expert witness used in my case was totally biassed in this way and I was told that if I don't like his report I would be welcome to bring in a second opinion but would have to pay for it myself, the sum of £5.000!

And then, there would be no guarantee that the second expert witness wouldn't be also in the same boat as the previous one, as the lawyers were on the same wavelength and mostly clearly double agents or too scared to contradict the churches.

Most survivors cannot afford their own independent expert witness, never mind go through a lengthy court trial against a clearly fascist driven methodology and vocabulary of a perpetrator church friendly hidden spider web of legal and PR armies.

Churches only ever respond or react to accusations, if they can no longer avoid it, be it due to a worsening public image, loss of taxes or legal proceedings.

The church leaders will only ever apologise but with no consequence, if they are forced to due to public or political pressure. And then they are only sorry for having been caught out.

They then will set up yet another charity or telephone helpline that simply look as a helpful and supportive measure but that are in reality intelligence gathering hubs and survivor entrapments that send them into circles like in a hamster wheel, instilling renewed false hope in survivors.

Such organisations and projects are always leading back to the perpetrator circles one way or another, when they f.ex. tell a survivor that their telephone line is only there to listen and to refer the victim back to the diocese to their very abusers, thus being abused yet again.

Those undercover charities and interest groups are always designed to disencourage the survivors to pursue any court cases they might bring forward. Sometimes, key figures that are really pawns of the churches and who have been placed strategically and with a lot of money involved pretend to be on the side of the survivors, will act secretly as deterrents for survivors.

They will have even been established as book authors, professors or experts in the disciplines involved in abuse research, and are known on social media, TV, on the writing circuit and with their engagements for survivors.

These are often perpetrators in disguise, whom the churches pick methodically, as they are blackmailed and easy to manipulate or to burn in the end, when they have fulfilled or failed their secret missions and purposes and the evidence against them is leaked.

In instances, when survivors were represented by a dedicated lawyer, the statements of the so-called expert witnesses were often totally disproved but sadly, the retraumatizing was done with the false statement, and should be compensated for as well as the reabuse.

Recommendations after inquiries are often only very slowly put into action, if at all. In the few countries, in which mandatory reporting now overrides the Confessional seal, and is now law, and where statutory limitations have been removed, it seems that since the older inquiries, like in Ireland, the churches have still found ways to escape their duties and worm their way out of compensation, reporting, and are continuing to use Mafia style strategies of Omerta and framing the innocent and witnesses and whistleblowers as before.

Court hearings are being sabotaged in whatever way of obstruction possible. Documents are shredded or disappeared; witnesses and their friends and families are threatened, bribed or even murdered.

There are very few politicians, who have stood up and are standing up for justice for the survivors.

Churches will often present concepts for safeguarding, intervention and prevention that are only half-baked in the intent to withdraw them again, as they won't work in reality and will be eventually lead to the closure of the charities or commissions that are supposed to enforce them, which are in most instances from old regrouped perpetrator circles anyway.

Chapter 14:

History repeating itself

Organised Child abuse and exploitation and related crimes are by no means a new phenomenon in the history book of the Roman Catholic Church, and later also of all other denominations.

Abuse, rape, enforced or illegal commerce surrogacy, trade with body parts, organs and human experimentation was rife and well documented over centuries.

Children and women were always treated like commodities by the churches, and the maltreatment part of the perpetrator culture. It is only in this century that more and more becomes public knowledge and we are in a position to compare notes worldwide in an instant via social media.

There are interesting pearls of documentation to be found in book jumble sales, for example about 'The End of Medieval Monasticism in the East Riding of Yorkshire', by the East Yorkshire History Society. The booklet features the abuse and rape and crimes committed in monasteries and even lists the names of nuns having given birth to babies as a norm, and monks having had relationships in the parishes - at the time of Henry VIII.

In another book about the experiences of the illegal dealings in London's morgues up to the 1990ies, 'Corrupt Bodies, Death and Dirty Dealing at the Morgue', by Peter Everett, we find out that bodies were treated like commodities and sold in parts by unscrupulous and corrupt forensic staff who were also supplied by nuns and monks with bodies they wanted to disappear.

It is meanwhile well established and documented, how religious orders cater for all sorts of organised criminality circuits under the protection of abused or hijacked or corrupt officials' seals of authority.

For example, a former Master of the Queen's Bench, a High Court Judge, helped cover up the organised crimes of his Freemason lodge, and only got removed after he was exposed with his various plots.

Social workers are often caught in the middle of greedy and seedy parties of paedophilia supply chains, or those of enforced adoptions and illegal human experimentation and secret societies. They are being fed with wrong information by the perpetrator circles, who often have official powers and status that they abuse.

It is well established, now also via the latest inquiry, the IICSA, that the churches can under no circumstances be trusted with child safeguarding. The various church figures have admitted it themselves that they are 'unable' and unwilling to enforce any disciplinary measures or mandatory reporting, if they had to by law.

We are reaching a boiling point, where you can hear the angry voices of past survivors of organised church criminality in various revolutionary centuries echo into this time, as the Vatican and Anglican Church, more recently also the Lutheran and the Evangelicals and Orthodox, still apply the same old silencing strategies but cannot stop the sheer flood of exposure of their crimes anymore.

The angry voices are now amplified again, and don't the churches hear them all to clearly in cold sweat by now, as even the popes are being thrown to their wolves now, and being dragged into the courts, and with them all their lose ends in the shapes and sizes of their cardinals, who are to each other liabilities.

With proof of evidence emerging from all corners of the world the process of ultimate justice and judgement day coming early is unstoppable and no more claim of deniability credible nor possible. 'Guilty as charged!' is the verdict.

Chapter 15:

The Devil's Advocates:
The double agents of the Churches

I was assigned a psychiatrist praised in his field of War Veterans PTSD Research, who was frequently acting as expert witness hired by the Catholic Church and the Inquiry.

He assessed my trauma and made an evaluation of my time at Croome Court. I was told and trusted him, as he was a famous professor and highly decorated specialist in his field.

He spent as little as two hours with me, after having to wait two and a half years to even get to see him and by this time my fellow friend and survivor John Lamb had already passed away without getting justice and closure for the abuse he had also endured.

Within his report the professor made incorrect assumptions about my family history and the causation of my trauma. He produced an inconsistent and biassed report which not only disrespected me but my deceased mother, father, brother, and sister.

He accused genetics and my impoverished home life as the main contribution to my traumatic life. Not the fact that between the ages of 10-16 I was in a care system that demoralised children, abused them in all unimaginable and unspeakable ways, and treated them like human punch bags all in the name of God.

When I received this report, I was shocked by the cliched and biassed statements he had made.

My father was a loving man who worked hard and struggled like many as a father of nine children living in Glasgow in abject poverty. He had enjoyed a good education financed by my great grandparents and he worked as a landscape gardener.

Against all the odds and the system that took children away from families to supply Catholic institutions with as many selected children as possible for their income source and for additional mercenary and many a secret or even illegal agenda he fought hard to get me out of the care system but was always refused because they deemed it in my best interests to be placed in the care of the authorities.

My sister who had also experienced abuse within the care system had children who had accomplished extraordinary things and attended high quality universities like Cambridge, St Andrews and Keele and have had amazing opportunities, as have mine.

So, if genetics did play a part in how you were raised and the path of your future, how have my children and my sisters and brothers' children been able to break the genetic assumption and exceed in life?

This report made me sound like me, and my family were the abusers and that I was destined and deserved the life I had been dealt. I protested this to my lawyer, and they said it didn't sound too bad, and it wasn't a reflection of my family.

They dismissed me and went ahead and let the professor submit his report. By this point I had lost all confidence in my lawyers as it was apparent, they didn't have the survivors as their priority but they seemed to have thrived on the accolade of taking on the Catholic church and to them it was just another feather in their cap.

Later I would find out that the majority of lawyers had been for decades double agents, who would accept fees from both sides, the surviving clients, and bribery from the churches, as these devil's advocates saved the Catholic Church the embarrassment of public exposure and, even more important to them, any court proceedings.

The Vatican will always make sure that expert witnesses and law teams are working against the survivors via strategies of delaying the justice process for as long as possible, and via ways of slandering the witnesses and victims, thus discrediting every single aspect the survivors might bring up.

It is a purposefully retraumatizing process, through which the church leaders, who are instructed via papal decree by the then Pope Benedict XVI. not to admit to anything under threat of excommunication, if they should report another clergy member's abuse, intend to discourage and frustrate the survivors from pressing charges and start legal court proceedings.

If the Vatican can no longer avoid inquiries or court proceedings and tribunals, they then spare no costs to hire the most recognised and expensive specialists that money can buy on their perpetrator friendly list.

We can see that recently in the former Pope Benedict XVI.'s choice of a London law firm, a top ten company in the world, and in my case, they chose an award winning psychiatrist, who specialises in the PTSD treatment of war veterans.

The Vatican makes sure that survivors have to go through their charity channels in order to get compensation or payment for therapy or these kinds of expert assessments. Thus it directly influences the outcome, as the pope wants to ensure that the survivors can be controlled in this way and the damage limited as much as possible.

In this way, the experts are only at face value impartial but in my case for example, the whole report was dismantled later again by new legal experts, who objected to every single statement and disproved them one by one.

It is beyond ridiculous and extremely tragic for survivors to be labelled like this and retraumatized. They have to live already under extreme duress and physical consequences on their long term health.

Every trigger results in also physical symptoms and ailments, like pain and fevers, tiredness and worse. To date I have received five apologies from the Catholic Church, these to me are just more empty words without any action.

'Sorry' doesn't change the past or the trauma that I am continuously living, and 'Sorry' doesn't bring back my childhood that was taken from me so cruelly.

In 2015 I received a postcard from Archbishop Longley sending his prayers and he at one point made a public apology at the inquiry but to this very day he continues with his colleagues to find excuses for the churches to not enforce the safeguarding procedures.

Cardinal Nichols, who was back then at one point also the Archbishop of Birmingham constantly justifies the non-enforcement of the new safeguarding in all religious orders as well, as he quotes that there are 'simply too many of them to keep track of'!

He and Archbishop Justin Welby have jointly at face value set up the One Church safeguarding policy, which is basically simply a regrouping of already known paedophile and CSA networks and means that combined spiderwebs are now being placed strategically in parishes of Anglican and Vatican churches with old veteran child abuse facilitators and trafficking enablers placed again as churchwardens, safeguarding officers, legal and data advisors, parish council members, parish secretaries and Sunday school teachers.

Even the IICSA confirmed in all its - albeit limited - reports that the churches can under no circumstances be trusted with their own safeguarding, and the passivity and refusal of the Chief safeguarding officer Nazir Afzal to even communicate and engage with survivors this is becoming increasingly clear.

From my experience with the Vatican I can honestly say I can't see any light at the end of the tunnel to justice. They will fight every survivor for as long as they can possibly get away with it, and with the dirtiest means available to them, too.

It is interesting to note though that survivors internationally have increasingly teamed up with scientists as well that are not linked to the churches and do their own investigations and that is a development the churches have not foreseen.

Nothing beats a 24/7 dedication of passionate justice seekers, who have learnt the hard way to cut off those, who have betrayed their trust and to connect only evermore with those, who are on the same wavelength, and share the same experiences all over the world.

It took Nazir Afzal, the chair of the CSSA, more than a year to even connect publicly with survivors on social media and only after evermore louder public outcry that he had ignored most survivors, who contacted him, and only ever interacted with those, whom he could control and who were still believing in building bridges to the church.

He proved already highly selective in the Rotherham trial, going after only a tiny group of offenders but leaving out many others, which suited the churches very well indeed, as they were looking for a chair for their pseudo safeguarding organisation, CSSA, whom they could control and drop, if necessary, again, should things go pear shaped and they would be held accountable for their failures anyway eventually.

One can already see now that there are further intrigues going on between competing Catholic charities and criticism is echoed suddenly against the CSSA, and especially against Afzal, by others, who have benefactors in Rome and want to replace him.

From where I am standing, I can see that there are so many warfaring splinter groups within the churches, who all want their piece of the cake of power and funding that the church is already a dead body, as it stinks rotten to the core from the head of corruption, organised criminality and fascism, never mind it will also one day be proven to have taught lies about almost everything and spread its arian heresy.

One can already see how the various church funded charities are fighting each other, all trying to make the most profit that then sustains a lot of pretend survivors, who are in this as double agents and spies and who are really perpetrators in disguise themselves.

Certain factions in the Vatican will stand up for their hidden agenda and only support the survivors that fit their secret plans and plots and others try to recruit and groom new victims from the pool of survivors that they lure into their charities only to retraumatize and abuse them all over again.

It is an encouraging sign and development that even a former Pope, Benedict XVI., sees himself suddenly legally challenged by a German court for failure to act. The survivor, who is suing the Vatican now on a new angle and loophole discovered by his out of the box thinking lawyer, forfeits his compensation in favour of the Vatican having to admit that crimes have been committed, which sets a precedent worldwide.

If he wins, survivors all over the world might be able to take the churches and other perpetrator organisations to court, even where statutory limitations were not removed, on the same approach to get the perpetrators and those, who covered up organised crimes like abuse, at least to admit to those crimes.

It is also bad timing for the Vatican, and especially for the popes and cardinals that the former chief auditor of the Vatican, Libero Miloni, is now suing the Secretariat of State for unfair dismissal and for compensation. All he did was being exceedingly good at his job, with decades of experience and expertise at Deloitte and the UN.

He uncovered more than the popes and cardinals had asked for to be found and his findings were evidence against Cardinal Becchu and the head of Vatican Police and many other cardinals, whose fraudulent transactions into millions of Euro were proven by Miloni.

Cardinal Becchu denounced Miloni as a spy to the pope in 2017 to prevent his own arrest but in 2020 the evidence nonetheless caught up with him, and he has to stand trial now. The Chief of Police had to resign and is not allowed to return to the Vatican.

There is one part of the perpetrator culture that is kept under lock by the IICSA as well as the media and the perpetrator culture, and I wonder why that is…

Namely the Freemasons, Templars, and other militant orders like the one of Malta, who are key players on behalf of the Vatican and Anglican churches worldwide. In fact, whilst at face value some of these organisations had been banned even by the Vatican or worldly powers and principalities, they are continuing especially since Pope Benedict XVI. and Pope Francis unhindered allowed them to exercise their hidden powers ruthlessly to obstruct justice against survivors, and to silence whistleblowers even literally.

There are now cardinals and arch/bishops emerging almost on a daily basis, who are accused and charged and proven guilty of all sorts of organised abuse and other criminality and of covering up church crimes for decades, whilst they were obstructing justice in any way they could and by also lying to investigations that they had no knowledge of any perpetrators and their crimes.

Chapter 16:

Lessons to be learned and Recommendations

As an ambassador to the IICSA's Truth Project I had handed in my statements and recommendations to the Inquiry. It was increasingly clear to me though later that the IICSA started to behave hostile towards me, when I began questioning their inaction and non-fulfillment of their legal responsibility in some cases that should have been reported to the authorities.

I asked Countess Sigrid von Galen for an independent report into Croome Court and other institutions that I had been placed in also on behalf of other survivors and she had a look at various inquiries in her preparation for the Independent ICJ Croome Court Report on behalf of us Croome Court survivors.

The IICSA Final Report was by no means as far reaching as the conclusions and recommendations of other international Inquiries into Child Sexual Abuse, like it was done in Ireland, for example, and more recently in some parts of the United States and in Australia.

Although Inquiries Reports are featured on leading TV and radio channels around the world and as front page news in the print and social media, court proceedings are still being sabotaged bluntly by the Vatican despite the removal of statutory limitations and mandatory reporting even having been made law in some countries.

Numerous survivors came forward to the various committees internationally. They all had suffered torture and abuse in institutions, including residential schools, work place schools, reformative and disciplinary homes, and orphanages.

It seems interesting that the remaining figures of witnesses actually testifying in the inquiries is drastically reduced for various reasons of which we already heard in the ICJ report.

Usually thousands or even ten thousands victims come forward, when a new inquiry is announced and in the making, but it is quickly filtered down in a mysteriously selective process by the chairs of board members to only hundreds of survivors, and the actual number of cases even ending up in a courtroom is even less than a hundred.

All the inquiries showed that the abused children were removed from their families and homes on a large scale and signed over by the bullied and legally ill equipped parents to social workers on behalf of Catholic and Anglican institutions with the authority of the education and Home Office departments of governments internationally.

There was always an element of networking in organised facilitation of child abuse, enforced adoption, illegal human experimentation, child trafficking, and child slave labour. These church and other criminal spiderwebs were abusing secret and public positions of authority and trust and also gave carte blanche to officials and caregivers for exploiting the children in any way under abuse of an official seal.

Hence many files, if they have not already been shredded or destroyed in other ways, are still kept under seal as classified because they show the corrupt intertwinedness of state and church collaboration for all sorts of purposes, many amounting ultimately even to crimes against humanity and state harm.

Children were and often still are viewed simply as commodity, the individual child persona completely ignored, and their needs utterly disregarded. Children had nowhere to go to complain or report abuse and other crimes.

They were cut off from the outside world, and if they were allowed or sent to congregations in the church or elsewhere, it was under the watchful eye of the nuns, priests, other staff and teachers.

And if they even made it to a police station and were brave enough to run away to actually get to talk to a police officer they were not even believed and sent straight back to the perpetrators' institutions.

At inspections the children were often sent outside, into the grounds or gardens or on assignments, so that they would be invisible and inaccessible for the social workers, who simply ticked the boxes without ever even having seen the children they were supposed to protect. The system of supervision and inspection was thus corrupt and fundamentally inadequate and flawed.

Children were abused on an industrial scale worldwide, of which the dimensions are only surfacing now, as the walls of silence are broken up by survivors, who at last speak out in ever growing numbers on a daily basis.

Not only have whole generations of children been failed in their emotional, physical and educational development - they grew up knowing only terror and fear every single day.

Boys and girls have been targeted in institutions from a young age, and were subjected to sexual abuse in pandemic proportions, whilst girls seem to have been abused by ringleaders and predators also to get them pregnant, including for surrogacy, and turn the baby into an object for enforced adoption, or as a commodity of the organ or body parts supply chain of organised church criminality.

Children did not know, whether they would live another day or when they would be raped, touched or beaten by one or more persons, who abused their trust on a regular basis.

If it was not them one day they had to witness others being tortured under screams.

Through the corrupt and dysfunctional inspection systems and a culture of Omerta the perpetrators got away with their abuse and other crimes for very long periods, and often even for decades, without being challenged for it. Hence it is almost impossible to estimate the ultimate numbers of victims. One can only have an educated guess at the rates and figures that are emerging now in various countries after the removal, either temporary or per law, of statutory limitations. In the United States for example we witness right now in some states the mushrooming of survivors coming forward for court proceedings against the churches.

Many survivors often remember their long hidden trauma only years or decades later and then need even more time after that to share their experiences with others. Most probably took their dark secrets and heart break into their graves without ever having told a single soul.

When the survivors finally came forward to reach out to the inquiries their voices were often silenced, as the churches aimed at keeping their cases out of the courts, or, indeed, kept them from the public wherever possible, as any disclosure meant possible compensation claims and damage to the reputation of the institutions and their perpetrator culture.

Religious authorities simply protected the perpetrators, and if it could not be avoided to penalise them, they would be moved on and transferred to a different church or institution, where they were free to reabuse yet again.

The popes knew about the dimensions and numbers of widespread sexual abuse but did all to keep the true level under lock. Investigations often led to empty vaults, if at all, to any results and it is happening to this very day that the popes deny the systemic proportions of abuse and fake their shock at the evidence, when it actually couldn't be suppressed or destroyed anymore.

The then newly elected Pope Benedict XVI. actually dictated an edict that threatened clergy with excommunication should they report a colleague for child sexual abuse. Cardinal Nichols even confirmed that at the IICSA that he rather excommunicated priests, who would inform on and report colleagues to the authorities after a confession.

That sums it all up and explains why the Vatican and Anglican One Church rather invests in a whole army of international lawyers, the devil's advocates, to bully survivors into NDAs than to have perpetrators charged and prosecuted in the courts.

He also had a secret agreement sealed with the late Queen Elisabeth II on his visit to Holyrood, that saw the two churches acting as One in pretending to protect and enforce safeguarding for children at face value, but that actually was a hidden proclamation to protect the perpetrators and hide them in each other's facilities and institutions, so that they would go unpunished and could continue to abuse unhindered.

Disciplinary measures and rules for breaching them are hardly ever enforced, neither by the churches nor by government departments, unless evidence is so strong and overwhelming that the officials can no longer ignore or suppress it.

More and more popes, cardinals and arch/bishops are now proven guilty as charged of obstruction of justice, intentful harm and crimes against humanity and of facilitating and being perpetrators themselves of organised abuse and other crimes and their cover ups internationally.

Joseph Ratzinger is now finally challenged legally of having been at least negligent in his time as bishop in Germany, but there are also insider Vatican sources, who place him in international court proceedings and arrest warrants for child abuse himself.

Police officers from Munich leaked papers that indicated that Ratzinger was abusing young boys in Munich but the investigating officers had been told to drop the charges and to scrap the investigations altogether.

A close friend of the Ratzinger brothers in Regensburg gave a statement that she knows that the Ratzinger brothers were part of a secret group of paedophiles and organised abuse. She and several girls from her class were also ritually raped, and the parents stayed silent, as they were part of the facilitating and enabling inner secret church circles. Some of the parents were also members or knights of various orders, like the Knights of Malta, and the equally notorious Knights of Columba.

These survivors' stories and black book police entries will one day come to haunt the popes as they are proof of these criminals disgracing and abusing the status of their offices from John Paul II. over Benedict XVI. and the present Pope Francis.

The latest revelations and vast numbers of organised abuse and other widespread church criminality are flooding in from France, California, Australia, Texas and of all mainly Catholic and Christianity orientated United States, South America, the Philippines, Germany, the United Kingdom, Canada, Poland, Portugal, Spain, Italy - the list is endless, and so are the perpetrator figures.

When will governments stop allowing the churches a special status of law and have the perpetrators finally prosecuted and stripped of diplomatic immunity? The neglect of the survivors amounts in many countries to dimensions and definitions of state harm!

Especially, as many Catholic orders now try to worm their way out of legal responsibilities, and/or the payout of compensation especially in historic abuse, by claiming that they were simply employees of or caregivers on behalf of Home Offices. How convenient to reject a survivor's application for compensation by referring them to the government instead, or indeed by initiating bankruptcy proceedings, so that the insurances have to pay out.

Chapter 17:

Life as a Whistleblower

Life as a survivor is one thing. Many survivors, like me, have carried the burden of their abuse all of their lives silently and with more or less grace and patience but also under great suffering quietly or by inner emigration in our souls and drowning our unspeakable memories and nightmares and pain and agony in alcohol or numb our minds even by medicine or drugs.

I will never forget the moment I decided to tell my family: We were watching the late night BBC news one Friday night, about a major investigation about the abuse in St Gilbert's Residential School run by the De La Salle organisation, also known as the Christian Brothers.

I was sitting in my armchair, together with my two youngest children, my then teenage daughters, in the front room, and we saw the images of St Gilberts on the TV. I felt such enormous relief, and gasped in excitement.

I was so happy that finally they were exposed, and I said to my daughters: 'See, I told you these Christian Brothers are evil! I was there as well and was abused! And finally people will believe me! Now the De La Salle organisation will be investigated at last! Nobody believed me, when I tried to tell them about their crimes!'

Once I had told my family, I felt great relief that they turned out to be really supportive and I wished I had shared it with them earlier. It helped them suddenly to make sense of my trials and tribulations in various stages in my and their life, as my actions naturally affected them as well. I am so very grateful for the love and closeness to my children and grandchildren.

I sincerely hope that many more survivors take a deep breath now and brave the odds and come forward as well with their stories to be heard as a result of this book. For far too long did we suffer in silence and felt powerless and disrespected and falsely classified and categorised, and not even believed, so much so that my whole life I often felt lonely, intimidated, tired of explaining myself, and disadvantaged and betrayed of my education and life expectations.

But I never gave up hope for justice and for the truth to come out. I am a fighter for the truth and my faith and human spirit are stronger than ever. I trust in God to see me through and I see all my suffering now in all those hell holes of Catholic institutions as a chance to help others out of the darkness that they have endured like me.

I am grateful that I did not turn bitter or unable to trust the people who are deserving of my trust, and that I learned to not trust somebody or an organisation anymore in advance but to let them earn my trust first.

As I said earlier, it is one thing to share your ordeal with your friends and family - it is an entirely new chapter and a whole game changer, when you decide to proceed to the next phase to serve the truth and justice as a whistleblower in order to help also others to free themselves of their suffering and to break down the evil walls of silence of whole organisations, especially if it is the walls of the Vatican.

As long as you stay in the system as a survivor to humbly ask for justice in the available channels, the Catholic Church (and the Anglican is part of it now as well as they formed the One Church Safeguarding collaboration, which is, of course, never being put into action, only at face value as explained earlier) will treat you with fake friendliness but will put you, make no mistake, into their strategic waiting loop like in a hamster wheel.

You will be referred to charities that pretend to listen and provide support to survivors but that never seem to go anywhere. Especially around the time of public inquiries they seem to mushroom everywhere, as the Vatican-Anglican churches want to find out as much intelligence by and about survivors as possible.

Telephone helplines and events for survivors are often their weapon and instrument of choice in this war of the Church against its victims, as a war it is, and every single exposure of the Church tactics are yet another battle to be conquered.

Survivors had to surrender too many times, lost too many battles to the Churches because we felt like David in the beginning of his challenge against Goliath but we have learnt to stand up, getting stronger with every momentary defeat, and we also grew evermore in the human spirit connecting and strengthening each other in our struggle and fight for justice on the path of truth.

We have passion for peace, justice and truth and we have a faith that popes can only dream of and that probably gives them nightmares of their own crimes against humanity. This faith and our hope in our victory of good over evil has always sustained us and has grown ever stronger.

As I felt supported by my family I started to encourage others to come forward, too, and to take the Roman Catholic Church to court.

When I started eventually to realise with many other survivors that we were actually just being played and artificially flattered by the churches in order to just keep us quiet and away from the courts I started to have a closer look and compare notes with the other survivors about all the delays in pay outs and even processing any claims, and the tactics of the Church seemed the same always and again all over the world.

We started to also look into which lawyers tried to bully us into NDAs and discovered a whole different silencing culture and perpetrator friendly side of the law professions that would do anything to help discrediting us survivors, so that we would not even dare to come forward with any claims.

I decided it is time to take the next step and start my journey in my wheelchair on a bigger road around the world for justice for survivors.

I became a whistleblower on social media that saves you real trips most of the time but gets your message across with one click, and it reaches instantly your fellow-survivors and those, who support us morally and with their knowledge and friendship and skills selflessly, all over the world.

When I started to be heard as I got more outspoken I was suddenly approached by the Archbishop of Birmingham, Bernard Longley, and by the Papal Nuncio, Claudio Gugerotti.

They met up with me and promised me to bring matters to the attention of Pope Francis and to help in the process of justice.

What PR stunts those were! They must have been clearly scared and keen to find out whether I was still intent to sue the Vatican and to make my case known, as it would publicly expose also the other institutions I was placed in, not just Croome Court that had links to government projects and files sealed until 2044 as classified.

I learnt in a short amount of time that the Vatican has different degrees of treating survivors like me - as they could not silence me with flattery and false promises and hamster wheel schemes and sent me in circles to frustrate and end all my efforts in the hope that I might die soon anyway, they started to place double agents amongst the panel of the IICSA, the lawyers, the followers on social media etc.

The moment the Vatican realised that I had become a whistleblower on a mission to bring out the truth in any case and to expose their institutions and their ways of retraumatizing survivors they began strategically to target me, like so many others, with all their efforts directed at silencing me and those, who would support me.

In the process, I met some fellow-whistleblowers, as you do, once you are on your mission and have devoted your life with passion to bring justice and lend your voice also to others, who are still voiceless, and I contacted Countess Sigrid von Galen, who has been a trailblazer and pioneer whistleblower against the organised abuse and other organised criminality and the fascism mainly in the Catholic and Anglican churches.

I am grateful that I met her just in time to benefit from her mentoring in regards especially to safety and security issues as a whistleblower, as the Vatican started to close in on me with their criminal cohorts and thus, I was able to prevent most of their attacks and let the Countess expose those tactics and strategies.

I let Countess Sigrid von Galen speak for herself here from her own experiences with the Vatican and Anglican churches, and also the Lutheran ones, as she was a target by all of them from birth being the secret granddaughter of Cardinal Clemens August Graf von Galen.

Our experiences and the attacks of the churches do overlap as well and together we decided to put these worldwide organised criminal institutions that disguise themselves under the smokescreen of the One Church on the map.

We decided to connect the dots here, so that the Churches' patterns of sabotage, obstruction of justice and of independent inquiries become visible and the hierarchy leaders accountable for their actions.

Their illegal activities are all too clear in their repetitiveness and universal abuse of authority and immunity, also looking back and rewriting the wrongs of the Vatican distorted and covered up history.

Countess Sigrid von Galen is also the first grandchild of a cardinal to publicly speak out about her appalling treatment by the Vatican and Anglican Churches, who tried to kill her on numerous occasions before she even did find out who her real paternal grandfather was.

But she had already started to write and expose the church and other institutions with a distinct voice nurtured by her various mentors in her teenage years, often wondering why so many strange coincidences happened in her life and why so many people wished harm upon her or offered to mentor her or tried to flatter her.

Her story will one day come out in her Memoirs but she wanted to share some of her experiences as a targeted whistleblower and surviving secret grandchild of a cardinal, who was about to expose the fascism and organised criminality within the churches, when he was murdered by the Nazi cohorts hidden by the Vatican five days after having been made cardinal in 1946.

'Let's just simply say here and now that the Vatican has a vast fascist paramilitary and mercenary killing machinery and its hierarchical structure serves this well, as it can draw on two thousand years of secrecy, infrastructure and command structures and deniability black ops since the remains of the Roman Empire, from which it learned to scout, train and awaken its sleepers in every generation, all in a well experienced perpetrator culture and under the law of Omerta.

Key leaders and individuals were lured into compromising situations, so they would do what they were told by the command structure, and that included also laity and children, and almost all were blackmailed via their secrets that they shared also in confessions.

If a target couldn't be flawed the Church found ways to discredit witnesses and whistleblowers, slander their and/or their friends and families' reputations, or to threaten them into submission.

If flattery or threats did not work, the Churches did and do not shy away from killing orders, of course, in deniability.

Ways of assassination or attempts thereof are for example poisoning, stabbing, arson, explosions, murder made look like suicide, embolies, car 'accidents', injected but untraceable overmedication, shooting,

The churches can draw on vast spiderwebs, secret societies, organised criminality clans, and open networks of charities that are run and protected secretly by hidden dangerous associations in joint enterprise, whose tentacles reach almost into every single neighbourhood worldwide.'

As long as witnesses, whistleblowers and friends and family members of whistleblowers are targeted by the Vatican and other churches, either through flattery, offers or bribery or threats, if the former fail, we shall expose these strategies whenever they are used against us.

'Throw stones at us', I say to the Popes, 'and we will throw back the boulders of the truth to get final justice and peace of mind'.

Chapter 18:

The Final Countdown to Judgement Day

The Doomsday Clock for the final countdown to judgement day is ticking for the Churches and all institutions and organisations that habitually abuse children in an organised systemic infrastructure.

It is only a matter of time now that the last walls of silence are coming tumbling down by the survivors, who break the silence and drag the truth into the open, never to be locked away again in anonymous vaults and places of torture.

There will come the time now, when children and parents point at the former buildings of the churches and their institutions and call them out for what they are and were: Crime scenes, now closed for forensic investigations and no longer be used as smokescreens for fake worship.

Sports heroes also will no longer be on the mountain top of the Olymp, as they will be exposed as abusers, rapists, and even murderers and greedy organised criminals, who happened to be chosen and promoted via a secret spiderweb of Freemasonry and other such secret societies.

Just walk around Covent Garden and you see the references of these dangerous associations and their joint enterprises in the public eye. Greed and lust for power is at the core of all of these organised criminal organisations from churches to football and sports institutions and of the individuals, who climb the snake ladders at the cost of lives and reputations and human dignity lost.

Was it worth it for these perpetrators to commit organised crimes only to reach the next step on the ladder and to gain yet another post paid for by blood and lies and betrayal?!

Chapter 19:

NEC LAUDIBUS NEC TIMORE - Countess Sigrid von Galen: The Granddaughter of the Cardinal: A life as a target of the secret Eye of Vatican Fascism and Organised Criminality

© Countess Sigrid von Galen

My grandfather was Clemens August Graf von Galen, and I am the cardinal's granddaughter - but I was only told this after my father's death in 2008.

Countess Sigrid von Galen at the age of four at St Lamberti
© Countess Sigrid von Galen

It was a shock that was lingering in my bones for several years before it settled as my grandfather's legacy and grew into my own burden and responsibility to spread the truth but the information instantly made my whole life appear in a new light and many questions I had often asked myself before were gradually answered, and I am still connecting many dots in history.

I have always been involuntarily in the focus of the Church and until 2011 I was also closely linked to the Catholic Church myself as a volunteer and on a professional basis. When I realised that the church was directly linked to all sorts of organised paedophile and other crime networks and to fascist movements I stopped going to church altogether.

My father, Clemens August Graf von Galen's secret son, Harry Wilhelm,
and my daughter Tiffany. © Countess Sigrid von Galen

The Catholic Church has long burnt all bridges for truth seekers
through its devious ways of fascism and organised crime, by making
life hell on earth for its victims, loose ends and whistleblowers.

Anyone who had eyes to acknowledge the real ongoings and also
asked how one could help victims of abuse was very quickly put on
the sidelines and the process of discreditation was put into motion.

© Countess Sigrid von Galen

This means, for example: assassination, death threats, poisoning, knife attacks, at you directed weapons, rigged operations, gaslighting, stalking, psychological warfare, torture, bribing and inciting crimes of those around, discrediting or removing witnesses, etc.

vLike with the mafia, these strategies are used under the law of omertà to silence the survivors and whistleblowers, thus always protecting the image of the church at any cost.

It speaks for itself that Joseph Ratzinger put an edict in place that demands the excommunication of any priest, who would blow the whistle on a fellow priest and would report a superior to the authorities.

I have personally experienced all these forms of intimidation because simply by birth I was a loose end to the Vatican as the granddaughter of a very well known and revered cardinal. It is only through the invisible protection of good powers that I am miraculously still alive...

I have always shared my gifts with my church family - as a solo singer, choir director, youth group leader, voice coach, voice therapist, TV/drama coach for theological shows, church events organiser and host to numerous church and parish events, concerts, exhibitions, luncheons, fetes and dinners, and I also served on the church council.

My life until 2011 was thus closely connected to the church. I have shared my gifts at my own table at home and in the house of Jesus Christ with enthusiasm and tireless dedication.

Until one day I realised that even in my then parish my trust was being betrayed again and children were being lied to, betrayed and, yes, sold too, via information exchanges of the various spiderwebs that pose as charities and church initiatives.

I've been writing about the abuse of power in the church almost 24/7 since 2006, when very few still gave a thought to the victims of violence and other organised crime in the church, but knew full well about it! And I was attacked for it from all sides, clergy and laity.

Word spread quickly in my church that I was not to be silenced.

© Countess Sigrid von Galen

I knew who tried to bribe children with gifts and invited them persistently on outings. And suddenly the hitherto friendly relations with bishops, church leaders, priests and deacons/nuns were all undone under excuses - or threats - by the bishops.

The children in the choir were even replaced for the last forthcoming choir retreat with children from other communities, who had been selected by churchwardens and the verger, who, as I found out later through the priest, belonged to various Paedophile exchange networks.

The priest, a whistleblower, sent me protection from these criminals and help in the form of an undercover police officer who posed as a representative of the music initiative that had provided the funding for the choir retreat and was supposed to assess our musical weekend.

After that, projects were cancelled or denied under cheap excuses, and I was told not to enter the church again with no explanation whatsoever, as that is yet another strategy to isolate whistleblowers from the community by giving no explanation but discrediting and cutting off their now loose end, who could spill the beans on the wider networks, and on the individuals involved.

The Catholic Church's abuse of power is particularly serious insofar as the Vatican can fall back on an ancient, well-rehearsed criminal infrastructure and a multi-disciplinary psychological and para-military warfare system in combination with the law of silence, the Omertà. Royal chaplains of the Anglican and Vatican One Church are also often involved in multiple roles as infiltrators and facilitators of child abuse and trafficking.

For example, in concrete terms, I was also strategically surrounded with selected people that the Vatican used as manipulators - as my fellow students, mentors, friends, neighbours, priests, bishops, teachers/professors/, spouses, godparents of my daughter, etc.

When they couldn't influence me not to speak out against the Vatican (either through interesting job offers or projects), then they started threatening me in various ways: with knives, staged car accidents, poisoning, or even threats to help my ex-husband take my daughter away from me by slander.

However, social services did not play along to the game of the bishop, who abused his seal of office, and took my daughter's statement seriously that the church community from which I removed us was full of paedophiles and murderous church leaders.

She had to witness how I was threatened with a knife by a church leader friend at a birthday party, and how I suffered from poisoning several times after Sunday mass!

The same befriended church family was also involved in stalking and slander and various organised criminal plots, for which they abused their father's OBE status of diplomatic immunity.

And they were just one part of a huge network, with international connections to Germany, Denmark, Scotland, America, India, St Helena and to many other countries.

Some church elders tried to warn me about the corrupt inner circles in the church, and some whistleblowers in religious orders and churches even travelled from abroad and gave me evidence of criminal and fascist motivated crimes committed by their churches and organisations, which I forwarded to the appropriate international law enforcement agencies and urged other Vatican victims/targets to do the same .

The time of bridge building with the church is long gone - I've tried for decades until 2011, and I see only regroupings and redistributions of power in the church since then, and no true discernment or humility nor the will to see justice through truth.

Ultimately, the popes are concerned with the new Roman Empire, which is based on lies and high finance. Joseph Ratzinger was the pope who purposefully used his alumni to push through the idea of the fascist Roman Church Empire.

He has tried not only to silence me because of being a loose end to the Vatican simply by birth but also because I persisted in exposing the truth. Only very few children and grandchildren of Vatican members are ready to stand up publicly for the truth. But the Vatican cannot silence its victims indefinitely.

His successor Jorge Bergoglio seems to be even more determined to kill off myself and who is even sending his cohorts also to my daughter and my friends and other family members to try desperately to silence us forever but we won't play along but continue to expose the lies and intimidation tactics and the already committed assassinations by the Vatican.

The Vatican is always ready to quote from the Bible, which the popes and their wolf packs in sheep's clothing of cardinals and bishops bend constantly in their favour and endlessly stretch even in the courts, if they suit their purpose but they rarely live up to their own standards the popes impose on others.

It is time for 'Alpha', a fresh start for a peace built on justice through truth as its solid foundation. And for 'Omega', the end of the organised crime and Aryan heresy of the fascist One Church of the Vatican and Anglican See.

'I am the way, the truth and the life' is Jesus Christ's motto to us!

My way is the truth, and it is the component in my breath and my blood that is keeping me alive.

Chapter 20:

When the Popes don't come to the Courts, the Starchamber comes to them

Warning: SATIRE

Where would we be without our childlike humour and stoic faith and hope and trust that in the end the truth will prevail and claim victory. If not in real life yet, we can speed up the process a bit by grasping the idea of putting the popes on trial in the Star Chamber, stripped of their immunity and deniability.

Star Chamber Exclusive:

Holy Counsel Mary Magdalene prosecutes,

By Countess Sigrid von Galen

Day 1 of the Trial against the Popes, previous and present:

MM: 'Joseph Ratzinger and Jorge Bergoglio! Would you care to share your innermost darkest criminal secrets with the Star Chamber?

I must remind you that God and Jesus Christ on their thrones and all of Heaven and Hell know them anyway but it will help your punishment, if you confess them voluntarily!

[Popes and all look to the hammer]

I can read your thoughts - you two would have used the hammer already to force a false confession out of your targets by slamming it on their knees.

You can consider yourselves lucky that we do not need to use such torturous methods to prove you guilty of organised Criminality, fascism, terrorism, artificially stirred up warfaring anyway schism and insatiable greed, not to mention even your lies and aryan heresy enforced with Omertà as your creed.'

[MM is pausing with an all-encompassing maximum sentencing in hell contemplation impregnated silence, which makes the two defendants nervously suppressing their gas relief. They are no longer able to keep still on their footstools in the dock]

MM:'You two and your predecessors, who will be tried posthumously and stripped of all their titles and honours and be wiped out of the Book of Life, have committed systematically and covered up internationally the most heinous crimes against humanity.

We shall hear about them here in the Star Chamber and you will have to listen to all the charges and witness testimonies, and you know as well as everybody present here that you are guilty as charged as hell!

Shall we ring now for the end of day 1 your special torture bell? Or would you rather voluntarily still before you are being led back into your cell already the truth tell?

I have removed your every curse and spell, so that you are simply visible as the two rotten apples that from their hellish orchard trees and from their own snake ladder fell!

You might recognise the nurse as one of your potential victims of attempted assassination.

I wish you well with her dedication and devotion to justice, and you can't anymore anybody manipulate or bully into a persuasion of paying compensation from their own purse!'

MARY MAGDALENE prosecutes:

WARNING: SATIRE

By Countess Sigrid von Galen

The Justice Gazette

The Vatican Trials

Day 2: Jorge Bergoglio

MM: 'Jorge Bergoglio! You are here in the Starchamber, where you have no immunity but are accountable with all your crimes against humanity and your responsibility for the organised church and wider Criminality and your cover ups under the code of Omertà!

You even offered in many cases an empty apology but with the intent never to act on it and with all promises you made for justice broken.

So, you intentfully deceived the public and your victims by using various cosmetic surgery image measures through setting up fake charities, helplines and pseudo-guidelines.

You know as well as we do that you only got away with your lies and smokescreens, never mind your heresies, which will be your smallest problems, once we have heard all the evidence against your Judas-Church.

You set up movements like Medjugorjie to gather intelligence and steal data and original work from genuine writers and even posed as other people on the internet under stolen identity.

You also continued Joseph Ratzinger's fascist spy network and para-military hidden in every country in church, politics, academia, and even the military, which he had expanded also with the Dalai Lama and inner fascist circles within international security agencies.

Religion was only ever the churches' smokescreen to rebuild a Vatican centred new world order.

I promise you that one of my sentencing suggestions for you and your church is to confine you to your own Vatican Roman borders as your collective prison, so that survivors and their families can point at it from the outside and say:'This is the most evil breeding place on earth!'

Chapter 21:

The Afterword

The Long Way To Justice is the ongoing journey of so many survivors and whistleblowers, and their families and friends, who were all targeted, abused, tortured, stalked, slandered, and many even murdered by the Vatican, Anglican and Lutheran Churches.

The story of Rafael Viola seems at face value very different from the life of a Countess Sigrid von Galen but we were both targeted and subjected to persecution and attacks by the Vatican and other churches and their secret dangerous and hidden political associations.

Rafael Viola was chosen for his unique skill set, multilingual and multicultural background by a well oiled machinery of child abuse, child trafficking, enforced adoption, illegal or secret human experimentation and torture that was facilitated for the sake and under the excuse of Cold War tactics by insider and outsider networks of the Vatican.

I am immensely grateful for Rafael's encouragement, support in manifold ways and the dedication to make this book happen.

Although I didn't even know that I was already known to and stalked by many as Countess Sigrid von Galen I was a target of the churches from birth, being the secret granddaughter of Cardinal Clemens August von Galen, the Lion of Muenster, who was murdered only five days after he became cardinal.

Clemens August Graf von Galen had realised that the Nazi enemy was hidden right in the Vatican and Anglican One Church infrastructure that was in lightspeed forced into action after WWII and that the

Allies were already forging a new kind of alliance with the Western churches against communism, their new old enemy.

My grandfather refused to be part of this new world order thought up by the inner fascist circles Western Allies and the Vatican and Anglican churches, and also to become possibly the first German Pope because the Vatican was by then an inner fascist circle within the One Church with seat in Germany, Rome and London;

He wanted to testify in a post war tribunal against the Nazis that were hidden by Pope Pius and who then became leaders in international allied secret services and intelligence agencies, the churches and in politics and science.

Once one starts to connect the dots and sees the smokescreens of religion and power fade into the spotlight of the truth, the real picture emerges, of how inner fascist circles in governments and churches have collaborated for decades after WWII to finish the war towards their new world order using the infrastructure of the churches.

What better disguise for the old giraffe and rat routes of the Vatican than a new pseudo-church - so useful for enforcing any political agenda and actively using the Vatican bank as an instrument for money laundering to keep the secret services in the Western hemisphere worldwide happy, and accomplices in facilitating the organised criminality and the paramilitary operations of the churches.

Files of corruption and abuse of power and of authority were conveniently sealed and loose ends simply murdered. The Vatican, Anglican and Lutheran churches could count on the seal of silence and on their status of diplomatic immunity in every single community.

Whistleblowers and survivors would be targeted in all ways to enforce the vaults and walls of silence. It is only more recently that survivors are able to exchange their experiences worldwide in an instant with one click, no matter where they are, no matter what their situation.

It is increasingly difficult for the perpetrators to hide and to silence whole scores of tsunamis of information from all corners of the world.

Our book and individual journeys and experiences are also overlapping with numerous others, who are still waiting for the right moment to speak out themselves but we are connected mysteriously and simply mind mapping.

We hope that this book is giving all those at last a voice, who are still voiceless and too scared to come forward. Rafael survived all his ordeals with a new strength that comes from living in the truth and having it shared tirelessly and selflessly.

I have been standing up for others all my life, too, and my family and friends have also paid heavily for it. It is for them, who suffered and gave their lives, that I can get up every day and fulfil my very own mission to give my voice to the voiceless.

Passion for the truth and to see justice being done for all survivors is our driving force and to see a survivor smile with peace in their heart is the greatest gift of all on this long way to justice.

May you thrive in the truth and see justice being done!

Yours

Countess Sigrid von Galen

I have come a long way from having been taken from my parents only to be sexually and psychologically abused, tortured and me and my family being assassinated in character by nuns and clergy and so-called expert witnesses to publishing this book about how the Vatican is stealing lives still from children to this very day out of greed and obsession with power under the smokescreen of religion.

It was only ten years ago that I at last started to share my trauma with my family and that I contacted the first lawyers to take the Catholic Church to court, which was a process of retraumatization in itself, which many other survivors share. Our stories are very similar but it is only a few of us yet, who dare to speak out.

I want to encourage and inspire those, who are still suffering in silence to also come forward and expose the crimes against humanity committed and omitted by the churches and religious orders.

There is a system in this organised abuse and wider criminality, and it needs to be visible to the outsider, as the exposure helps to disrupt and dismantle the hidden dangerous associations amongst the Vatican and Anglican churches, both of laity and clergy, and also the involvement and protection by governmental hierarchy.

Be bold and don't fear to speak the truth! Only the truth is the key to justice and ultimately to inner peace. We deserve healing and to be looking forward to moving on with our lives.

Having experienced the lies and denial of responsibility and the numerous broken promises by highest ranking Vatican representatives I have enough of their inaction and active obstruction of justice and their refusal to surrender their perpetrators to the courts.

This book is my legacy to other survivors to encourage them to continue speaking out until justice is served!

My faith never faltered and I still can trust those, who are worthy of my trust and are tirelessly helping me to expose the smokescreens of organised Vatican Criminality.

Always remember that the word of the truth is the sword of justice! I am grateful that the Countess answered my plea for exposure of the hidden organised criminality of the churches, as we share our fate in many ways, although different in nature.

Every survivor of church abuse: You are in my thoughts and prayers! Carry on the torch and be a beacon of the truth!

Yours

Rafael Viola

GLOSSARY

(Keywords, Names and Places of Mention)

A
Archdiocese of Birmingham
Assault
Assessments

B
Bergoglio, Jorge
Birch, Arthur
Bisson, Jonathan
BND
Brook, Peter

C
Catholic Safeguarding Agency
Charities
Child Abuse
Child Sexual Abuse
Child Sexual Exploitation
Christian Brothers
Church of England
Churchhouse
CIA
Clemens Sisters
Clergy Abuse
Codes
CoE
Commission to Inquire into Child Abuse, Ireland
Compensation
Corruption

L
Legal loopholes
London Diocese
Longley, Bernard

M
Mandatory Reporting
MeTooChurch Movement
Memory wiping
MI5
MI6
Military Agencies
Mind Programming
MK-ultra

N
Nafzal, Azir
Nichols, Vincent
Nocivelli, Dino

O
Oetken, Angelika
Omerta
One Church
Organised Church Criminality
Organised Criminality

P
Papal Nuncio
Perpetrator Culture
Pope Benedict XVI.
Pope Francis
Pope John Paul II.

R
Rape
Ratzinger, Joseph

RCC
Roman Catholic Church
Ryan, Sean

S
Sabotage
Secret Societies
Sisters of Charity of St Paul the Apostle
Sisters of St Margaret
Social Services
St Chad's Cathedral, Birmingham
St Gilbert's Approved School
Statutory Limitations

T
Templar Knights
Tennal Assessment Centre
The Independent Commissioner for Child Sexual Abuse Issues (UBSKM)
Torture

U
UBSKM
United Nations

V
Vatican
Vojtila, Karol

W
Welby, Justin
Westcott, James John
Westminster Cathedral
Westminster Diocese

Z
Zollner, Hans

Further Reading:

Connelly, John, Echoes of the Past, Author House, Bloomington, 2008

Cooper, Teresa:no2abuse.com

Countess Sigrid of Galen,Hear their Voices, London 2022

Countess Sigrid of Galen,The Granddaughter of a Cardinal, London 2022

Countess Sigrid of Galen,Nuns are the Smoking Guns, London 2022

Countess Sigrid von Galen, P.S.:The Catholic Church Abuse and Anglican Report, London 2021

Countess Sigrid of Galen, jamesjohnwestcotthouse2.blogspot.com

- Clemensaugustvongaleninstitute.blogspot.com
- Countessigridvongalen.wordpress.com
- Sigrid-von-galen.blogspot.com
- ello.co/countesssigridvongalen

Cross, Claire,The End of Medieval Monasticism in the East Riding of Yorkshire, East Yorkshire Local   History Society, 1993

The Institute for Criminology and Justice (ICJ), Independent ICJ Report: The Anatomy of   Sabotage at International Inquiries into Child Sexual Abuse, Author: Countess Sigrid von Galen, London 2022

- The ICJ-List of free law libraries and resources for research, compiled by Countess Sigrid von Galen, London 2016
- ICJ Report 8/2016: CoE and RCC Crimes against humanity under abuse of diplomatic immunity, Author: Countess Sigrid von Galen, London 2016

- ICJ Report 2019: Child Abuse and Child Trafficking by Secret Societies, Author: Countess Sigrid von Galen, London 2019

Mills, Patrick: patmills.wordpress.com

Viola, Rafael:Rafael Viola's Blog:

heartheirvoicescroomecourtrafaelviola.blogspot.com

- https://ello.co/rafael1viola

Printed in Great Britain
by Amazon

26453957R00069